HOW
OUR RELIGION
BEGAN

by

EDNA M. BAXTER

Drawings by

EDWARD F. DUGMORE

HARPER & BROTHERS PUBLISHERS

NEW YORK · LONDON

HOW OUR RELIGION BEGAN

To the loving memory
of my mother

3

CONTENTS

vii

CONTENTS ix

CONTENTS

Charts

FOREWORD

This book has been written for youth above the age of eleven. It may serve as a book for the home or as a course for juniors, intermediates, or seniors in the church school. For teachers, using this book as a course of study for pupils between the ages of 11 and 18, an edition is available with a final chapter giving teaching suggestions and bibliographies.

Because an appreciation of the Bible and of its religion are so dependent upon an understanding of the development of religious ideas, particularly ideas of worship and of God, laymen who teach or are parents may also find this book of great value for themselves. By far the most thrilling approach to the Bible is that of the development of religious ideas. To study the Bible in a developmental way clears up obscurities, gives perspective on primitive concepts, and leads to an appreciation of the noble religious heights reached by later Jews and particularly by Jesus.

Many have contributed to the preparation of this book. To all who have, the author wishes to express her gratitude. Particular thanks are due to Professor A. J. William Myers for his encouragement, to Professor Moses Bailey for reading the manuscript and for his scholarly criticisms, to the late Lewis B. Paton and to his wife, Mrs. Lewis B. Paton, for their critical scholarship, to Mrs. Willard T. Carter and to Professor Frederick S. Hynd, Director of the Hartford Art School for guidance in the work of illustration, to Amy Clowes for teaching some of the material in the author's Junior School of Religion, to Lynn Burns for typing the manuscript, and to all others who have assisted in any way.

Special thanks are due to Charles Scribner's Sons for permissions to quote from *The Dawn of Conscience* by J. H. Breasted, and from *The Heroes and Crises of Early Hebrew*

History from the Creation to the Death of Moses, by Charles F. Kent, and from *Poems of Van Dyke* three lines of "The Friendly Trees"; to The Pilgrim Press for permissions to quote from *The Early Religion of Israel,* by Lewis B. Paton, from the *Pilgrim Boys and Girls Quarterly,* October, 1926, "A Song of the Exiles," from the *Pilgrim Elementary Teacher,* January 1935, "Shabbas Cheer"; to The University of Chicago Press for permission to quote the play, "Ruth," by Elizabeth Miller, from *The Dramatization of Bible Stories;* to the Presbyterian Board of Christian Education to quote the letters from the author's Junior Departmental Graded Course of January-March, 1931, and of October-December, 1930; to Harvard University Press for permission to quote from "The Harvard Theological Review"; and to the International Council of Religious Education for permission to quote passages from the "American Standard Bible." Unless otherwise designated, the Biblical quotations are from this source. My sincere thanks are also due to Harper & Brothers for their gracious permission to quote from the Moffatt translation of the New Testament, and to D. Appleton-Century Company for a brief quotation from *Experience with the Supernatural in Early Christian Times,* by S. J. Case.

Thanks are due to the following for permission to make line drawings from illustrations: American Sunday-School Union for drawings taken from *Archaeology and the Bible,* by Barton; the British Museum for drawings from ancient monuments; a capstone from a pyramid found in *Histoire de l'art Egyptiens;* the Palestine Explorations Fund for a drawing from a photograph of a high place at Gezer; the Dayton Art Institute for the use of their photograph of Nofretete; The Metropolitan Museum of Art for the use of a photograph of a bas-relief of captives being led to Ashur-nasir-apal and also a drawing from a picture of a caste of Ikhnaton; and the Oriental Institute of Chicago for drawings from an altar of incense from Megiddo, the Ishtar gate of Babylon, the Egyptian winged sun-disk, and a pottery shrine from Megiddo.

HOW OUR RELIGION BEGAN

CHAPTER I: FINDING GOD

Everyone living today owes a great debt for almost everything that he has to millions of people who have lived in the past. Christians and Jews today owe a very great debt for their religion to the Hebrews and their neighbors who lived many hundreds of years ago. Most of our religious customs and our religious ideas have a long and interesting story. There was a time when people had no temples, no synagogues, and no churches. Today when we go to our churches and synagogues, it is very important to remember how great this debt is to millions of people who have lived before us.

When we pass the various churches and synagogues it may remind us that people do not all think just alike about religion. If we travel in other countries we will find enormous temples and unusual religious customs practiced by millions of people, quite different from those of our own churches and synagogues. Today we believe that all peoples in all lands have been seeking God and trying to find answers to their questions about the mysteries of the universe and about life.

People have tried to explain birth and death, the growth of trees and plants, the reasons for floods and for disasters, the causes of sickness and disease, and many other things. Always they have given answers that were connected with the gods or with spirits. It seems as if they have been on a long quest to know the truth and to know God.

As time passed and their knowledge grew, we find peoples' answers to their questions changing. At the same time as their ideas of the world changed, their customs of worship and their ideas of God have slowly changed.

In this book we are going to tell the story of some of the

fascinating beginnings of the Hebrew religious customs and beliefs, especially those which may be found in the Old Testament part of our Bible.

Scholars have learned many things about the beginnings of the Hebrew and Christian religions from the Bible. They have also made wonderful discoveries from ancient buildings in Babylonia, Palestine, and Egypt.[1] Many things have also been learned from the customs of desert people who live in Arabia today, much as the ancient Hebrews lived there thousands of years ago when they were nomads.

This is a Semite whose head was carved on stone and shows how the neighbors of the desert Hebrews looked.

LIFE IN THE DESERT

Both Jewish and Christian people find the beginnings of their religion in and near the great Arabian Desert. Thousands of years ago the people who lived around this desert were called Semites.[2] If you should look into the oldest parts of the Bible, you would find references to such people as the

[1] See Chapter XXIII for a more complete story of how we learn from the past.

[2] G. A. Barton says that Arabia is the center from which the Semites spread. Among the Semites were the Babylonians, Aramaeans, Canaanites, and Hebrews and today there are the Arabs and Ethiopians.

Canaanites, Assyrians, Babylonians, Ethiopians, and Hebrews. These were all Semites, but as they settled in different places they came to have different names. The ancestors of the people whom we know today as Jews were Hebrews of the long ago. They also were members of this early family of Semites who wandered about with their flocks in the desert and lived in tents.

Vast stretches of the Desert of Arabia offered the Hebrews nothing but burning sand and rocks in the midday. There was nothing growing but parched shrubs. The night brought coolness and a covering of sky and stars.

As they were needed, the tribes moved their flocks, camels, tents, and families to find water and growing things. Both man and beast were cheered by the sight of an oasis. Today, as then, water bubbles up from a spring in the midst of the sand and gives refreshment to thirsty caravans. Trees provided fruit and shade.

At the close of a journey or when a new home was found the black tents were taken from the backs of camels and set up until a city of tents had been arranged. Women did much of the work of setting up the tents. They also prepared cheese and gathered wild fruits. They made pottery jars and dishes in which to carry the water and to prepare the food. With hand looms they wove cloth for their loose garments and for their black tents.

FINDING ANSWERS WITHOUT BOOKS

Four or five thousand years ago, when the ancestors of the Hebrews were nomads in the desert, they did not have books or schools or libraries or teachers or scientists. It was necessary for them to discover everything about the world and about religion for themselves. Sometimes they learned from their neighbors in Babylonia and Egypt. Most of the things which seem quite simple to us were very wonderful discoveries when they were first found out. Imagine living in a world

without any fire to cook your food or to keep you warm. Then
perhaps you can feel the greatness of the discovery of fire and
fuel. Try to think how you would answer questions if you had
to start at the beginning of things. What would you think
makes the sun rise in the morning? What makes the stars come
out at night? What makes it rain? What makes trees and
flowers grow? What is the thunder and the lightning? Remember that there would be no books, no teachers, and no scientists to help you.

Just as people today try to find out answers to their questions, so did the people called Semites in those faraway days
try to understand the wonderful world around them. Life is
really a very difficult thing to understand. Before there were
any scientists to help people to explain it, the Semites thought
that breath was the spirit inside of people. They believed that
when people died or even when they had dreams, there was
a living spirit which left the body and visited distant places.
So they came to think that ghosts[3] were superior to men and
they feared and honored them as superhuman beings. The
Semites called them by the name ēl, or the spirit of a person
who had died. Ēl is the oldest name we know, meaning god
to the Hebrews. An ancient name for the Hebrew nation is
Isra-el which tells of something which ēl did for his people.

Just as they thought that there was a ghost or spirit living
in people, so they began to believe that there were spirits living in trees, rivers, wells, stones and mountains. Everything
that moved or had life seemed to show the power of a god.
In Canaan where the Hebrews later came to live the people
called these spirits by the name "ba'al" which means "owner."
The plural of this word is baalim. There was a ba'al of the
frost, a ba'al of the dew, a ba'al of the thunder, a ba'al of the
storm, a ba'al of trees, a ba'al of springs, a ba'al of mountains,
and a ba'al of stones—a ba'al for each. All of these things in
which a god or ba'al dwelt were known as "beth-el" which
means "house of deity."

[3] Read Job 4:12-17. The word "ghost" refers to a spirit. Read I Samuel 28:13.

The movement of the sun, moon and stars, the floating of clouds, the crash of thunder, the flash of lightning, the rustle of leaves, the flowing of water, were believed by early people to be alive and to possess a spirit.

Here is what the ancient Babylonian neighbors of the Hebrews said about their gods:

> The highest walls, the thickest walls, like a flood they pass.
> From house to house they break through,
> No door can shut them out, no bolt can turn them back.
> Through the door like a snake they glide,
> Through the hinge like a wind they blow.

The early Hebrews, like the other Semites, knew very little about religion and life as we know it today. They were wrong in some things which they believed, as, for instance, when they thought that the wind was made by some spirit blowing hard. When a stream flowed gently they said the spirit was asleep and when the stream was disturbed they said the spirit was angry. They could only think of things happening in nature because of something which was alive and doing these things. They knew nothing about the laws of nature and at first they were far from realizing that there is but one God.

Yet these early people were preparing the way for us to know about the world and the way God does work in it. To them we owe our belief in one God. We may not agree with their first ideas but we must remember that in the long future people may not agree with us. The universe is so vast that it seems as if man could never catch up with all there is to learn about it and about God.

Longfellow once wrote a beautiful poem about the Indians called "Hiawatha." In it he says that the people long ago were finding out something about God all the time.

> Ye whose hearts are fresh and simple,
> Who have faith in God and nature,
> Who believe that in all ages

Every human heart is human,
That in even savage bosoms,
There are longings, yearnings, strivings
For the good they comprehend not,
That the feeble hands and helpless,
Groping blindly in the darkness,
Touch God's right hand in the darkness
And are lifted up and strengthened:—
Listen to this simple story,
To this song of Hiawatha!

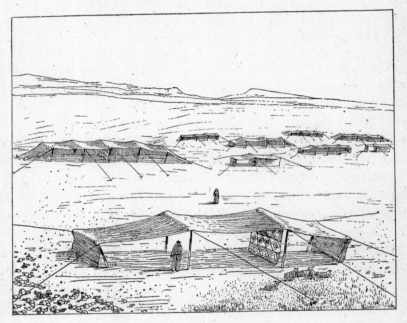

The early Hebrews like all nomads of the long ago as well as the Arabs of today lived in black tents woven by hand from the hair of black goats.

THE DESERT WANDERINGS

Thousands of years ago, the tribes of desert people in Arabia often wandered with their flocks into the fertile country along the rivers. It was natural that these people should seek the rich pastures of river valleys where they could find food for themselves and their camels, goats and sheep. On the northeast of

Arabia, some settled along the Euphrates and Tigris rivers. Cities grew and later we read about them becoming the powerful countries of Assyria and Babylonia. Other Semites left the desert to settle in the northwest near the Jordan River. This country was called Canaan. People settled along the Nile River and this became the great country of Egypt with its enormous pyramids and temples.

The Hebrews continued to live around the Arabian Desert for many hundreds of years. In these times their customs and beliefs were like those of other desert people. Even today we find Arabs living around the Arabian Desert in black goats' hair tents with flocks of sheep and goats and their camels much as the Semites lived thousands of years ago. The ways of this desert have not changed very much.

In the Bible there is a very ancient story of a Hebrew tribe led by Abraham. With their sheep, goats and camels the Hebrews wandered into the city of Ur. Later they went north and east from Ur to the land of Aram, and settled for a time in the city of Haran. Haran belonged to the kingdom of Babylonia. Over it ruled a king called Hammurabi who is famous for his great laws. He lived about 2200 years before Jesus. Perhaps the Hebrews learned something about these laws for their own government later on.[4] The cities of Ur and Haran, probably offered this Hebrew tribe many good things in trade for their wool and sheep, but they were true sons of the desert and preferred to live in their tents and wander around with their flocks on the edges of Babylonia.

Their numbers increased and this always led to a new search for land for their flocks. They heard of good pasture in the beautiful country of Canaan over by the Great Sea. It was "a land of wheat and barley, and vines and fig trees, and pomegranates; a land of olive-trees and honey" (Deuteronomy 8:8). Some of this tribe came here to dwell.

As the Hebrew tribes increased in number there was al-

[4] See Chapter XXIV for a fuller account of these laws.

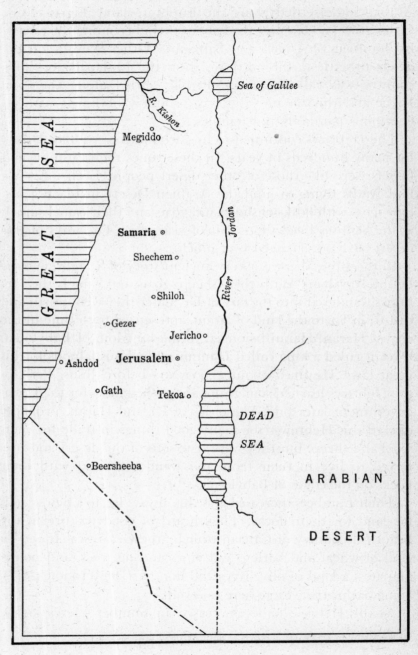

No. 1. Palestine

ways need for greater pasture lands. Perhaps some of the tribes settled in Canaan in very early times, but many of them remained nomads or wandering people. We know that some of the Semites later were called Canaanites. They settled in Canaan and built cities there at least two thousand years before Jesus was born.

There is a story in our Bible about a Hebrew tribe under Jacob going to Egypt to live during a famine in Palestine. Between fourteen and twelve hundred years before Jesus, these Hebrews who had been living in Egypt fled from their taskmasters and again sought new pasture lands. They pressed into Canaan and fought against the Canaanites until finally they came into possession of much of the land. After several hundred years in Canaan, the Hebrews slowly gave up many of their desert ways of living.

THE HEBREW STRUGGLE IN PALESTINE

After living many years in the land of Canaan, the Hebrews finally conquered it. They had many struggles to keep it because their more powerful neighbors in Egypt, Assyria, and Babylonia sometimes sent armies to take it from them.

In 586 B.C.[5] the Babylonians did take it from them and only the poorest were allowed to remain. The leaders and skilled craftsmen were carried away to live in Babylonia. After the exile, as we call it, these Hebrews, together with those who were left behind, became known as Jews.

Later on the Greeks and then finally the Romans came to govern Palestine. So we read in the time of Jesus that the country was governed by the Romans.

In A.D. 70[6] the city of Jerusalem was destroyed by the Romans and the Jews were scattered. Today they live in many parts of Europe and in the United States. Several thousands have returned to Palestine to live, but the Arabs who have al-

---

[5] B.C. after a date refers to the years before Jesus was born.
[6] A.D. refers to the years after the birth of Jesus.

ways lived there do not welcome them. The story of the Jews in many countries has been a sad one because the people have not always wanted them. Yet it is to the Jewish people that Christians owe most for the best and noblest ideas in their religion. Christians are particularly indebted to this great people for Jesus who was a Jew, living and worshiping as the Jews did in Palestine, nearly two thousand years ago.

What Do You Think?

Directions: Put a cross before every sentence which you believe is true.

1. God is like an old man.
2. God is like the very best father.
3. To show love for God it is necessary to have love for people.
4. God dwells in people.
5. God was once a god of war.
6. God wanted the Hebrews to kill their enemies.
7. God spoke with a voice long ago.
8. Sometimes God gets angry.
9. Once God enjoyed the sweet odor of animal sacrifices.
10. Long ago God desired the Hebrews to offer children in sacrifice to him.
11. God prefers goodness more than offerings.
12. Once God lived in an ark.
13. God is only to be found in churches.
14. God depends on people to bring about better living conditions.
15. God depends on people to learn and to use health laws.
16. God loves bad people as much as good ones.
17. God sits on a throne up in the sky.
18. God works through orderly laws.
19. God has not changed, but people have changed in their ideas of God.
20. We have glimpses of God when people are helpful and full of love towards others.
21. God never takes revenge nor becomes angry.
22. Where love is, there God is.
23. God did not love the Philistines and Egyptians as much as the Hebrews.

24. Frequently innocent people suffer because of the mistakes or the selfishness of others.
25. The law of love is one of God's greatest laws.
26. God depends on people to learn to co-operate with Him in building a better world.

Something to Do

1. Write down your own idea of God and then do it again after you finish this book. What part do you think God has in the life of trees and plants? What part do you think God has in storms, floods, and earthquakes? What part does God have in matters of disease and health? What part does he have in wars?
2. Write down some questions about religion for which you would like to find answers.
3. Imagine yourself living in the desert with the Hebrews four thousand years ago. Then make a list of things which you now have that you would have to give up. Make a list of questions that you would want answered if you were living at that time.
4. Try to think of things in our religion for which we are indebted to people of the past.
5. Put check marks before the test, "What Do You Think?" If you have any more questions about God, add them to the ones which you have already written down.

CHAPTER II: SACRED WELLS, SPRINGS, RIVERS, AND WATER

THE IMPORTANCE OF WATER TO DESERT PEOPLE

The worship of water in springs, wells, and rivers is very common among many people and easy to account for, since water is so precious for the life of plant, animal, and man. Because wells, springs and rivers appeared to move and to be alive, it seemed as though they contained spirits.

Let us try to imagine how important water would be to people in the desert. The ancestors of the Hebrews lived in and around the Desert of Arabia. This country is a thousand miles long and about six hundred miles wide. It is a dreary land with rocky mountains separated by unwatered plains. Only a few thorny plants can grow in it. There is almost no rainfall, and there are no rivers. The only places where things can grow well are in the oases where the water comes up out of the ground and makes a spring.

Try to imagine the early Hebrews on a journey in the desert wilderness of Arabia. They are crossing over high stretches of flat rocky land walled in by hot mountains of bare rock and finding nothing alive except some thirsty herbs and a few grey and thorny acacia trees. Suddenly coming to the top of a ridge, they behold a new world. Camels, flocks, and people quicken their pace and soon they are under a canopy of stately palm trees spread out to give them shade against the blazing heat of the sun. Ground water rises to the surface and provides a carpet of green and growing plants. There is drink and refreshment for beast and man. Is it surprising that these early Hebrews supposed that this was the dwelling place of an ēl or a spirit? Is it surprising that these nomadic people of long ago approached a well with ceremonies of worship?

An oasis in the desert.

SACRED WELLS AND SPRINGS

In Arabia it was believed that the water around the palm trees in the underground stream was inhabited by a god, ēl, or spirit, responsible for the springs, streams, and underground flow.

The Hebrews referred to flowing water as "living" water. To them it seemed as if a spirit made it move. In one of the oldest bits of Hebrew poetry, the well or fountain is addressed as a living being:

> Spring up, O well; sing in response to it,
>   Well that the princes digged,
> The rulers of the people delved
>   With their scepters and staves!
> From the desert a gift!
>   (Numbers 21:17,18)

This old song of the well is said to have been sung at Beer

in Moab. It suggests that some important chief had dug the well and sung songs to it. In this very same place today Arabs have been found practicing the same custom. This is what they say:

> Spring up, O well;
> Flow copiously
> Drink and disdain not
> A staff have we dug it.

Probably when the ancient Hebrews came to the well, they called to the spirit to let him know that they were coming. Then they danced around the well singing songs.

For centuries nomadic people have come to this well of Beersheba for water.

Sacred wells are among the oldest objects of reverence among the Semites. In Palestine, to this day, springs are considered the dwelling places of spirits. Peasant women, whether Muslim[1] or Christian, ask the permission of these spirits before

[1] Muslim people follow Muhammed, who lived many hundreds of years ago, instead of Jesus.

drawing water. The people of Palestine have often believed that they could be healed of their diseases at some of these springs.

At another place called Katanā there is a spring where people come to get cured of fevers. Wheat is thrown into the spring as a gift to the spirit in it and the people say, "O Allah, wilt thou accept this sacrifice?" Sheep and goats are sometimes killed here as an offering to the spirit and the people eat them with the spirit.

SACRED RIVERS

The Semites like many other primitive people supposed that spirits lived also in rivers. When they saw the land beside the streams made ready for growing things and providing them food, they felt that a spirit must be living in the water. Rivers in Palestine have been held sacred for many hundreds of years. The river Tripolis in that land is still called a holy stream. At its source is a grove which is sacred to both Christians and Muslims who live near it. You see how firmly people cling to old beliefs even though they change the name of their religion. Even in our churches in America you may discover people who believe in old superstitions.

In seasons when the streams dry up, a feast is held at the source of the river in order to persuade the spirit to make it flow again. Sometimes at certain seasons of the year the river Tripolis is made red by the soil. The people in Palestine once explained this color as the blood of the god who lay buried at its source in the Lebanon Mountains.

Many people besides the Semites have worshiped river gods. There are people in other lands today who think that there are river gods. In India, one of its greatest rivers is the Ganges. It is fifteen hundred miles long and its sources are in the glaciers up in mountains about thirteen thousand feet high. One of the gods of the Hindu people in India is called Vishnu. They think that he helps mankind and gives life. They say that the river Ganges springs from his feet. Because this great river makes the land fertile, it seems as if it were the work of their god, Vishnu. Since many people of India have never seen the source of the Ganges it is easy for them to think that it comes from the feet of Vishnu. Such ideas have made the Ganges a sacred river and multitudes of Hindu people come to bathe in it, expecting that it will do them good.

A tribe of American Indians called the Chippewas also think that spirits dwell in streams. Sometimes the Grand Medicine Society will sit beside the water for hours at a time, singing their religious songs and beating a drum hoping for instructions from mermaids or supernatural animals who are believed to dwell in the stream.

There are certain Chinese people who feel that the great Yellow River is inhabited by a dragon who is the god of the river. When the river gets low or dries up, they say that the god is angry and so they perform ceremonies and hold feasts to persuade this dragon god to send rain again. They also suppose that it is the dragon god which makes their crops grow, and so they worship it.

For hundreds of years there were people who said that he who bathed in the spring at the source of the Euphrates River would be free from sickness during the whole year.

If you read in your Bible the story of the Garden of Eden you will discover that the Hebrews in this ancient story had the idea of a garden planted by a god and watered not by rain but by rivers.[2]

In the countries around Arabia, successful crops depend more upon the water supply than anything else. So it happened that land watered by a stream was said to be inhabited and owned by a spirit, or ba'al. Moving water in a stream, the fall of rain or its absence, all these natural processes seemed to indicate the presence of a god. The Semites did not under-

[2] Read Genesis 2:8-10.

stand the causes of rain. This led them to depend on river spirits in order to get good crops. They worshiped these gods in order to win and to keep their favor. Even the early Hebrews did this when they came to live in the country or Canaan because they knew no other way to be certain of good crops.

Something to Do

1. Why do you suppose primitive people would think water in the desert or in a moving stream was inhabited by an ēl? Try to read some of the ideas of the Egyptians in *Stories of Ancient Peoples*, by Emma Arnold, pages 9-11.

2. What knowledge do we have today that changes such religious ideas?

3. Read some incidents in the Bible where Hebrew people told stories, showing that they believed their diseases could be cured by bathing in a stream. See II Kings 5:9-14. John 5:2-7 and John 9:7. How do you suppose such stories started?

4. Are there people today who expect to be healed by bathing in rivers? Try to find out about the customs in India, in connection with the river Ganges. Read Chapter 12 in *Finding God*, by G. W. Taylor.

5. How do people today expect to be healed of disease? Do you know any people who expect to be healed by other methods than those which science has discovered? Science is finding out more and more about the laws of disease and of health. What do you think is the relation of God to these laws? What does man have to learn to have health? If people are ignorant of germs or health laws does God protect them from disease?

CHAPTER III: FLOODS

FLOOD STORIES

Great disasters like floods and earthquakes have always been difficult for people to understand. Today we are learning more and more about their causes and, as we do, we cease saying that God sends them to punish us.

In many countries folks have told stories of a great flood by which all the people on the earth were destroyed, with the exception of one or two favored persons who were saved in some miraculous way. The ancient Hebrews also told a flood story which is recorded in the Bible in the Book of Genesis, Chapters 6 to 8. In these old flood stories the disaster was often explained as punishment or at least as being sent directly by the gods.

This is the image of the sun-god worshiped by people in the city of Babylon.

BABYLONIAN FLOOD STORY

A story that is much older than the Hebrew one in our Bible was told in Babylonia at least two thousand years before Jesus was born. This is the way these Semites explained a flood:

It seems that the god Bel was very angry with people everywhere and made up his mind to destroy all of them. When Ea, the god of wisdom, learned of this, he gave warning in a dream to a man called Sisuthros, who was one of his favorites, that Bel was sending a terrible flood. Ea directed him to:

> ". . . build a ship
> Leave goods, look after (thy) life,
> . . . . . .
> Cause all kinds of living things to go up into the ship;
> The ship which thou shalt build,
> Let its form be long;
> And its breadth shall equal its length;
> On the deep launch it."

The directions to Sisuthros are much like those given to Noah in the Bible story, except that it is another god directing a man called Noah. Sisuthros carried out the directions given him by the god, Ea. He built the ship and then took into it many kinds of food and drink. He says:

> "I brought on board my family and household,
> Cattle of the field, beasts of the field, the
>   craftsmen,
> All of them I brought on board."

When the rain began to fall, Sisuthros entered into the ship and closed the door. The flood became so terrible that even the gods were terrified.

> "The gods, bowed down, sat there weeping
> Close pressed together were their lips,
> For six days and nights
> Wind, flood and storm overwhelmed the land
> But when the seventh day arrived
> . . . . . .
> The sea became calm, the tempestuous wind was still,
>   the flood ceased.
> Then I looked for the race of mortals,
>   but every voice was hushed,
> And all mankind had turned to clay
> As soon as the light of day appeared,
>   I prayed
> . . . . . .

After twenty-four hours an island rose up,
The ship approached the mountain rises,
The mountain rises caught the ship and held it fast

. . . .

When the seventh day arrived
I sent forth a dove and let it loose,
The dove went forth, but came back;
Because it found no resting-place,
    it returned:
Then I sent forth a swallow, but it came back;
Because it found no resting-place
    it returned:
Then I sent forth a raven and let it loose.
The raven went forth and saw that the waters had
    decreased.
It fed, it waded, it croaked, but it did not return."[1]

When Sisuthros learned that the land was dry, he built an altar on the top of the mountain to offer sacrifices to the gods.

"Seven and seven bowls I placed there,
And over them, I poured out calamus,
    cedar wood and fragrant herbs,
The gods inhaled the odor,
The gods inhaled the sweet odor,
The gods gathered like flies above the sacrifice."[1]

The god Bel was angry when he discovered the ship and that there were men still alive. But Ea pleaded with Bel, and told him that he had helped Sisuthros because he was a good man and that only wicked people should be destroyed. Ea suggested that instead of sending a flood it would be better to increase the lions and hyenas, and to send plagues and famines to kill evil people. After Ea had reasoned with Bel, he ceased his anger. Bel touched Sisuthros and his wife, and made them gods and took them above the earth to be with the other gods.

THE HEBREW FLOOD STORY

If you will open your Bible to Chapters 6, 7, and 8 of Genesis, you may read a story very much like this ancient one

[1] Kent, Charles Foster: "The Heroes and Crises of Early Hebrew History," p. 59.

from Babylonia. In the Hebrew story it is a god named Yahweh[1a] who despairs of people because of their wickedness and who decides to send a flood to destroy them. Yahweh selects Noah and his family as the best people to be saved.

Noah was given full directions by Yahweh to make a box-like boat about four hundred and fifty feet long, seventy-five feet wide, and forty feet high. This boat was to be built like the Babylonian houses and to be watertight.

After it was finished, Noah was directed to take pairs of every kind of animal and bird acceptable to the Hebrews, together with all the members of his family, and enter the ark.

Then the rain poured down for forty days and forty nights until all living things on the land were destroyed. At the end of the forty days Noah sent forth a dove, but it returned. He waited seven days longer and once again sent out the dove. This time the dove came back with an olive branch. The third time he sent forth the dove, it did not return. Then Noah knew that the waters had gone down.

Noah came forth from the ark and made a great sacrifice of many animals to the god Yahweh.

"And Yahweh smelled the sweet savor; and Yahweh said in his heart, I will not again curse the ground any more for man's sake . . . neither will I again smite any more everything living, as I have done" (Genesis 8:21).

MODERN EXPLANATIONS OF FLOODS

There have been floods in many countries. One of America's worst floods was in the Mississippi Valley in 1927.[2] Thousands of hungry, cold people were driven out of their homes by this great river, rushing angrily to the sea and carrying away everything in its course. Perhaps some of these people also thought that God was sending the flood to punish them for evil deeds, somewhat as the people had long ago.

[1a] Chapter VIII of this book tells about the Hebrews learning to worship Yahweh.
[2] In the *National Geographic Magazine* for September, 1927, Vol. 52, are pictures of this flood.

There are today, however, many people who understand the causes of floods. They know that heavy rains in thirty-one states and also in parts of Canada were the real cause of the Mississippi flood. Much of this water found its way into brooks and rivers and on into the Mississippi River. Another important cause of this flood was the fact that too many trees had been cut down so that there were not enough roots to drink up the rain. The water had to find its way into the rivers and became so deep that it overflowed their banks and caused great destruction.

People have not always understood the orderly ways of the universe. They have often believed that great disasters such as floods were sent by the gods to punish them. Even today there are some people who still believe this. Engineers tell us that we have enough knowledge today to stop floods in America if people would work together to use it. Scientists are teaching us more and more about ways to obey the laws of the universe. Teachers of religion are teaching us how to work together to obey these laws so as to help God care for His people. Many intelligent men and women today believe that God depends upon His people to overcome difficulties, to discover the laws of His universe, and to learn to use these laws. When man loves his neighbors enough to use the laws of the universe to help them, many disasters may be prevented.

Perhaps that is what some Americans are just beginning to realize when they are planting more trees and building dams to care for the flood waters.

Jesus said that God sends the rain "on the just and the unjust" alike. Perhaps the people who explain floods as an act of punishment by God are mistaken. Both good and bad people may suffer from floods unless they learn the causes of them and work together to prevent them. This will mean that people who are not living in flood sections of the country may need to help those who do to change the conditions that bring these disasters.

Before the hills in order stood,
Or earth received her frame,
From everlasting thou art God,
To endless years the same.

—*Isaac Watts*

Something to Do

1. How do people explain floods today? Try to find the *National Geographic Magazine* for September, 1927, and read about the great Mississippi flood in the United States.

2. Write to the Department of the Interior, Washington, D. C., and ask for some material showing how the United States government is trying to control floods.

3. Read the Hebrew story written three or four thousand years ago to explain a flood. It is found in Genesis, Chapters 6, 7, and 8. In a book by Louis Wallis, *God and the Social Process,* you will find two flood stories from the Bible, on pages 318-322.

4. Compare the Hebrew story with the Babylonian story told in this chapter. In what ways are they alike? In what ways do they differ? What do both stories say caused the flood? What are the gods like in these stories?

5. You may read some interesting flood stories told by other peoples in the little book, *Finding God,* by G. W. Taylor.

6. How does your idea of God differ from the ideas of these ancient peoples? Take a paper and divide it into two sections. On one side place primitive ideas of God and on the other side place the nobler ideas of God which you are discovering.

7. How did the ancient gods seem to feel toward people who displeased them? What did Jesus think about God's attitude toward people who had done wrong? Read a story which Jesus told, in Luke 15:10-32.

CHAPTER IV: SACRED TREES

From the very earliest times in Canaan, the land we call Palestine, there have been people who believed that spirits lived in certain trees. The Hebrews and other Semites came to these trees to bring offerings to the spirits in them. Sometimes they came to these holy places to get healed of their diseases. There is a grove of trees in Palestine today, where people come every year at Easter time and at the harvest time. Those who are sick pray to the god and say, "If I get well, I will bring a sacrifice."

Without any science class to teach them the causes of leaf and flower and fruit bursting forth from the tree, early people explained them as the sign of an indwelling spirit. Even today in Palestine there are sacred trees and groves where an unseen power is felt to be in possession, guarding and protecting everything placed within the enclosure. Plows and agricultural implements are often left by their owners near a sacred tree or groove for greater security. So great is the fear of the tree spirit that no one would ever steal the things left there.

TREE WORSHIP IN OTHER PARTS OF THE WORLD

After the long winter, the tree with its appearance of lifelessness bursts forth into leaf, and flower and fruit. Primitive people, hearing the creaking boughs and murmuring leaves and seeing all of the changes taking place at different seasons in the tree, explain these things as the sign of an indwelling spirit.

People who think this way often dislike to cut down growing trees. The Ojibways say it causes pain to the tree. Some

Filipinos will not fell certain trees because they believe that the spirits of the dead dwell in them.

The Siamese offer rice and cakes to the takhien tree before they cut it down. An Austrian peasant asks forgiveness of the tree before felling it. The ancient Roman farmer, before cutting away trees, fearing the anger of the spirits, tried to win their favor by offering sacrifice and prayers. (Turn to page 114 to read about the ceremony for cutting down a grove.) Some Greeks, today, still believe in tree spirits. It is reported that Greek woodsmen throw themselves on the ground face downwards as the tree trembles before falling, lest the spirit see them and punish them.

All life is mysterious. People of the present and of the past have tried to explain it. Sometimes primitive man thought that he had originated from trees as well as from animals. There are many interesting myths of this belief. The Greek one tells how the god Zeus made a race of men from the ash tree. The Norse story says the sons of Bor made men out of two trees. One of the famous kings of Mexico was said to have come from two trees.

Educated people today are still impressed by the wonder of life and growing things but do not explain it as primitive people do. Scientists have taught us much about the way trees grow, how their buds develop and are preserved throughout the winter, and how they are nourished by the earth and the sun. Possibly you may wish to experiment and find out some of the thrilling things about the way trees grow and develop. After you have made these discoveries, perhaps you will be impressed as much or even more than primitive man by the wonder of it all. Today there are many people who think that there is one great spirit or God creating life wherever it is. This God works in orderly ways and man must learn to work with Him. He accomplishes His purposes best when people learn the laws of His universe and co-operate with them so as to create ways of love and friendliness.

The heap of stones suggest that the tree is sacred.

SACRED TREES IN THE BIBLE

The earliest records in the Old Testament are full of references to sacred trees. When the Hebrews came to live in Canaan they followed the customs of the older inhabitants. The gods of the Canaanites were located at certain sacred spots and when people came to these places they worshiped them.

Slowly the Hebrews began to worship Yahweh at these ancient sacred places. Later on when Hebrew writers told their stories of their earlier heroes, they often connected them with some experience with Yahweh at a sacred tree. In a very old legend we read that Yahweh appeared to Abraham under a sacred terebinth at Moreh (Genesis 12:6), and again at the terebinths of Mamre (Genesis 18:1). Another story tells that Gideon was called to his work by an angel of Yahweh "under the terebinth which was in Ophrah" (Judges 6:11).

There is a curious legend about Moses' experience with a sacred tree in the land of Midian. One day while he was leading the sheep of his father-in-law, Jethro, towards Mount Horeb, an angel of Yahweh appeared in a flaming bush and spoke to him. The angel commanded Moses to go back to Egypt and help to deliver the Hebrews from the oppression of the Egyptians (Exodus 3:1-13).

Another ancient Hebrew story tells about Deborah, a

prophetess, and says that "she dwelt under the palm-tree of Deborah between Ramah and Beth-el in the hill-country of Ephraim: and the children of Israel came up to her for judgment" (Judges 4:5).

During the war between David and Saul we read that "Saul was sitting in Gibeah under the tamarisk-tree in Ramah, with his spear in his hand, and all his servants were standing about him" (I Samuel 22:6). Later on the story says that when the Hebrews discovered that Saul and his sons had been killed, they burned their bodies and then "took their bones, and buried them under the tamarisk-tree in Jabesh, and fasted seven days" (I Samuel 31:13).

Dreams were considered a very important method of communicating with the gods and with Yahweh. One time Jacob is reported to have received a favorable message from Yahweh in a dream. When he awoke he said, "Surely Yahweh is in this place; and I knew it not." He was terrified but he "rose up early in the morning, and took the stone that he had put under his head, and set it up for a pillar, and poured oil upon the top of it. And he called the name of that place, Bethel (the house of an ēl): but the name of the city was Luz (almond-tree) at the first" (Genesis 28:18, 19).

During a war between some of the Hebrews and the Philistines, David regarded the wind in the mulberry trees as an omen or sign of Yahweh's help. The story says that "it shall be, when thou hearest the sound of marching in the tops of the mulberry-trees, that thou shalt bestir thyself; for then is Jehovah gone out before thee to smite the host of the Philistines" (II Samuel 5:24).

In all of these ancient legends of the early Hebrews we find evidence of sacred trees and the association of a god with these places. Even after the religion of the Hebrews had outgrown many forms of ba'al worship, they continued to think of the presence of Yahweh at certain special places such as springs, caves, shrines and trees. Sacred places or holy objects were regarded as dangerous to approach or to touch. A holy place was not only mysterious but had powers which were dangerous. It could be approached safely only by fulfilling very carefully certain prescribed conditions. Holiness in these early days did not mean goodness but separateness of the god. There was a sense of dread and fear when the worshiper approached a holy place. At the burning bush Moses was warned to remove his shoes because the spot was "holy ground" (Exodus 3:5). When Jacob awoke from his mysterious dream at Bethel "he was afraid" (Genesis 28:17), and he set about to pour oil over the stone. When the Hebrews first worshiped Yahweh at Sinai, we find that they were warned not to approach near enough to see Yahweh lest they perish (Exodus 19:21).

Out of this belief in sacred places and the fears associated with them, grew up very elaborate customs and ceremonial laws. By carefully observing these laws primitive people felt that their relations with the gods would be safer and more profitable.

About 745 B.C. we find the prophet Hosea denouncing some of the Hebrew religion of his day because of worship "under oaks and poplars and terebinths" (Hosea 4:13).

Devotion to these old sacred places seems to have continued until after the time of Jesus when the great temple at Jerusalem was destroyed in A.D. 70.

There were many leaders among the Jews after the exile who came to believe in one God of the whole world, as well as a God of goodness. For such people these ancient holy places were no longer necessary in the worship of God. To them holiness came to have a nobler meaning. Instead of aloofness, it came to mean purity, goodness and mercy.

By the time of Jesus we find him saying "God is a Spirit (John 4:21, 24). Paul says, "Know ye not that your body is a temple of the Holy Spirit which is in you?" (I Corinthians 6:19). These ideas of God found in the teachings of Jesus reveal the great change in the thinking of the Hebrews from the time when they worshiped an ēl or spirit in a tree.

How fair are the trees that befriend the home of man,
The oak, and the terebinth, and the sycamore,
The broad-leaved fig-tree and the delicate silvery olive.
—Henry Van Dyke

Something to Do

1. What do you think makes trees grow? Have you ever seen an acorn and then noticed the tree beside it, that grew from a similar acorn? What is there mysterious or wonderful about this process? How would you explain the growth of a tree?

2. Why do you suppose primitive people thought that spirits lived in trees? Read Chapter 23 in *The Childhood of the World*, by Edward Clodd.

3. Read the fascinating story of "The Gold Mohur Tree" in *Totaram*, by Irene Mott Bose.

4. How would you explain God in connection with trees or plants? What changes have scientific discoveries about plants, trees and nature made in man's idea of God? Write down primitive man's idea of God and beside it in a parallel column write down a loftier idea of God that may come with a better understanding of nature.

CHAPTER V: THE GROWTH OF RELIGION IN EGYPT

While the Hebrews were living as nomads or wanderers around the Arabian Desert, their neighbors in Egypt were doing many thrilling things. For thousands of years the Egyptians had lived along the river Nile. Here they built enormous temples and pyramids. Here they were discovering many wonderful things about the world and about religion.

Today, people are just beginning to learn about this marvelous civilization in ancient Egypt. They are discovering the treasures of art that have been hidden in their tombs for so long. On the pyramids, temples, and tombs they are reading their curious picture writing and learning about their customs and their religion. In this way we are discovering that the Hebrews probably learned some things from the Egyptians and so we are interested in finding out about their religion too.

THE LAND OF EGYPT

Egypt has a very old and wonderful history. Thousands of years before America was discovered, or even before our ancestors were civilized, the Egyptians were living in an advanced society. The climate was not too hot and not too cold. There were many sunshiny days so that people needed clothing to protect them from the heat rather than from the cold. From the flax the Egyptians learned to make linen of marvelous fineness.

Because Egypt was a land where it was easy to get a living, the people had time to discover how to do many things. They measured time and planned a calendar. They were the first people to understand surveying.

Since the Nile River passed through the center of the country, Egyptians learned to make boats for travel. After a time

A glimpse into the great Egyptian temple of Karnak.

they became skilful enough to make boats that could travel on the seas. Travel by sea helped ideas to spread.

People who go to Egypt today are amazed to see the great temples, statues, and pyramids, some of which the Egyptians built five thousand years ago. These monuments are among the chief wonders of the world. The Egyptians learned how to move, over great distances, enormous stones weighing several hundred tons. These were used to build magnificent temples for their gods and great pyramids as tombs for their kings. Some of the pyramids were made of millions of blocks of stone each weighing a ton or more.

THE GODS OF EGYPT

Like other early people, the Egyptians did not know the natural reasons for the change of seasons and the other processes in nature. They supposed that there were gods who managed them. They worshiped the Nile-god, Osiris,[1] because this great river gave them water for their crops. They worshiped the sun-god, Ra,[2] because it was thought that crops depended upon his kindness.

The sun-god, Ra, was considered one of the most powerful of the gods. People in many other countries have also worshiped a god who looked after the sun. Our own ancestors must have worshiped the sun because the first day of our week is named Sunday.

The Egyptians imagined several things about Ra. Some pictured him in human form ferrying across the heavenly blue ocean or sky in a "double reed-boat," with the stars as his sailors. In many parts of Egypt the sun was thought to be a hawk flying across the sky each day. So the symbol for this god was a sun disk with the outspread wings of a great bird or falcon.

[1] An interesting story of Osiris may be read in Wells, M. E., *How the Present Came from the Past*, Book II, pp. 195-99.

[2] A story of Ra and Osiris is given by Taylor, W. G., *Finding God*, pp. 70-76.

It was said that the enemies of the sun were the rain, the storm, and the clouds. In an ancient temple we find there were people thinking that the sun-god caused life and growth. They said, "Thou hast driven away the cloud, and hast expelled the rain, and hast broken up the clouds."

In the Bible, we find mention made of the Hebrew god, Yahweh, and words used to describe him that are like those used for the sun-god of Egypt: "the wings of the morning" and "the sun of righteousness . . . with healing in his wings." These words referring to the wings remind us of the Egyptian symbols for Ra.

The sun-god of Egypt was often pictured as a falcon with outspread wings.

Gradually the Egyptians began to regard their sun-god as the chief of the gods. The Egyptians said that he was a god interested in people and no longer a god of nature. They gave him the new name, Ptah. Ptah was said to have created the other gods and to help in the affairs of people.

PYRAMIDS

Just how much the Egyptians reverenced the sun-god is shown by the tombs which were built for their kings. Some of the rulers (the Pharaohs) spent a large part of their lifetimes and an enormous amount of money building tombs to preserve their own bodies after death.

These tombs were enormous pyramids which were lifted high above the earth to greet the sun-god. The top of the pyramid was higher than all other buildings and was the first object to receive the rays of the sun, which glittered on its polished peak and sides.

A door in the pyramid led to a temple where it was supposed that the spirit of the dead king could come forth to receive and enjoy offerings which were prepared by the priests for him.

These offerings were of many kinds and were very rich. It was thought that the things used by the living were also necessary to keep the dead alive in their world. So offerings of food, drink, clothing, ointment, perfume, and incense were made by the priests for their departed ruler.[3]

On the side of the capstone of one great pyramid facing the rising sun, we find a sun-disk with wings over a pair of eyes which seem to represent the eyes of the king buried below. Beneath the capstone it reads, "The face of King Amenemhet III is opened, that he may behold the Lord of the Horizon when he sails across the sky."

When the priest presented these offerings to the spirit of the king or the Pharaoh he entered the mysterious chamber behind the court of the temple and stood before the great door leading into the pyramid. Standing here, the priest spoke to the king as if he were alive and presented to him a rich collection of gifts. After each gift he repeated special words and at the close of the offering, said, "Given to thee are all offerings, all oblations, even thy desire, and that by which it is well for thee with the god forever." Finally the priest performed some charms to keep away hunger from Pharaoh. Sometimes he gave recitations for his pleasure.

THE KING IN THE SKY

There seems to have been the idea that the king not only lived in the pyramid tomb but also in a heavenly place for the dead up in the sky. This reminds us of the beliefs that Chris-

[3] See pictures in the *National Geographic Magazine*, May, 1928.

tian people have sometimes had of heaven. Perhaps some of the later Christian ideas can be traced back through the time when the Hebrews knew the Egyptians.

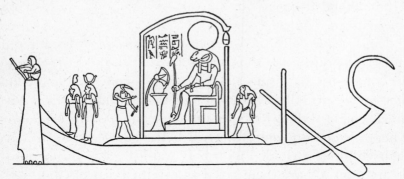

This is the celestial boat of Ra, the sun-god of Egypt. This god, with a head like a ram and wearing a sun-disk, is seated on a throne in a chapel. Thoth stands before him like an earthly king.

Writing on the old pyramids has given us many interesting things about the Egyptians and their religion. Sometimes we find that the dead king was considered to be one of the stars. Other writings describe him living with the sun-god, or even becoming the sun-god himself. On one pyramid it tells about the king bathing with the sun-god and being served by less important gods.

In the land of Egypt with its blue, cloudless sky, it is not surprising that the people, beholding the stars in the splendor of the nightly heavens, thought that they were their departed kings passing across the sky.

In later times the king was regarded as the earthly son and representative of the sun-god, Ra. So quite naturally, after his death, the king went to join his father in the sky.

PURIFICATION BY WATER

Before the king could ascend to the sky to live with the sun-god, Ra, it was thought necessary for him to perform certain ceremonies to purify himself. One way to purify himself was by water. Sometimes offerings of water were poured out to the gods. Other times the king bathed in a sacred lake, where the gods provided him with towels and sacred garments to wear. This method of preparing oneself for the gods is a very old oriental ceremony.

People have continued the custom of using water for religious purification for thousands of years. In our churches we use water for baptism. Though people continue to be immersed or sprinkled with water in their churches, they have slowly changed their ideas about the meaning of the ceremony. There are some people who still believe it necessary to have their children sprinkled with holy water by a priest or minister in order to have them saved and in the favor of God.

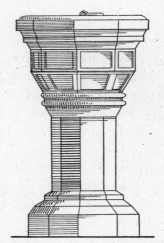

When people are baptized with water in their churches, they promise to devote their lives to the ways of God.

In other churches parents have their children baptized as a promise to God that they will help them to become His worthy followers. Water is used in baptism in many such churches as a symbol of purity.

THE KING ASCENDS TO THE SKY

After the baptism or purification by water the Egyptian king flew like a bird to the sky and was ferried across it to the sun-god. You may read some of the things which were written thousands of years ago on one of the old pyramids.

This king Pepi flies away from you, ye mortals. He is not of the earth, he is of the sky. . . . This king Pepi flies as a cloud to the sky like a falcon, this king Pepi reaches the sky like the Horizon-god (Harakhte).

As he arrives in their presence, there is much questioning by the gods and finally the king is received into the sky to be with them.

THE GODS BECOME NOBLER

Slowly the Egyptians changed their ideas of the gods. Instead of their being merely gods of nature they became gods who assisted man in his living and were interested in his goodness. Here are a few of the teachings which have been preserved after thousands of years. These are much older than the teachings of the great Hebrew prophets, yet at times they remind us of their ideas as we find them in our Bible.

Exalt not the son of an important man above an humble one, but take for thyself a man because of his ability.[4]
If thou speakest the truth in thy house the nobles who are over the land will fear thee.[4]

More acceptable is the virtue of the upright man than the ox [made as an offering] of him that doeth iniquity.[5]
Do righteousness that thou mayest be established on earth. Comfort the mourner, afflict not the widow, deprive not a man of the possessions of his father. . . . Be not harsh, kindness is seemly.[5]

On the doorpost of the tomb of a government leader

---

[4] Breasted, James H., *The Dawn of Conscience*, p. 155.
[5] *Ibid.*, p. 156.

(Ameni) in ancient Egypt we find words that were probably addressed to the sun-god:

There was no citizen's daughter whom I misused, there was no widow whom I afflicted, there was no peasant whom I evicted, there was no herdsman whom I expelled. . . . There was none wretched in my community, there was none hungry in my time. When years of famine came, I ploughed all the fields of the Oryx barony [his own lands] . . . preserving its people alive, furnishing its food so that there was none hungry therein. I gave to the widow as to her who had a husband. I did not exalt the great (man) above the small (man) in anything that I gave.[6]

So we find that the Egyptian and other rulers were beginning to feel that justice and goodness were important in their religion. The sun-god had begun to require his followers to live the good life. "It is an abomination of the god to show partiality."[7]

Rulers must be just and right because it is desired by Ra, the sun-god. Ra says "Speak truth, do truth . . . for it is great, it is mighty, it is enduring."[8]

On an old coffin have been found some noble words which were supposed to have been said by the sun-god: "I have made *every man like his brother*, and I have forbidden that they do evil, (but) it was their hearts which undid that which I had said."[9] In the land of Egypt, nearly two thousand years before Jesus came, we find people thinking that all people were equal in the sight of God.[10]

We find the sun-god, Ra, growing more and more interested in living people. Gradually Osiris, the god of the Nile River and the god that gave life to growing things, took the place of the sun-god and became the judge of people after death. His realm was under the earth and he became the king

[6] *Ibid.*, pp. 213, 214.
[7] *Ibid.*, p. 216.
[8] *Ibid.*, p. 219.
[9] *Ibid.*, p. 221.
[10] Jesus taught very much about God being the Father of all people and loving everyone.

of the world of the dead. Just as plants revived and came to life, so it was supposed that the king became Osiris and rose from the dead as Osiris had done.

Later on it was thought that Osiris arose and was lifted to the sky. We find some confusion in the beliefs about Ra and Osiris.

Something to Do

1. What were some Egyptian ways of thinking of God?
2. Would you like to make a classbook on Egypt containing pictures of life there and some of the religious ideas found on tombs and temples? The following books will help you:

   Finding God, G. W. Taylor, pages 70-76.

   How the Present Came from the Past, M. E. Wells, Book II, pages 195-199.

   The World We Live In, Gertrude Hartman. Chapter VI.

   National Geographic Magazine, May, 1923; March, 1926; September, 1926; and September, 1913.

   See also Chapter VI in this book.
3. Try to find pictures in other numbers of the *National Geographic Magazine* on ancient Egyptian life.
4. Perhaps you would like to know why people are baptized in different churches in your community? Why are people baptized in your own church? Were you baptized? Ask your parents to tell you about it. What was the purpose of this ceremony?

CHAPTER VI: SOME EGYPTIANS BELIEVE IN ONE GOD

Perhaps the most wonderful things that happened in the growth of the Egyptian religion were the teachings and reforms of the Egyptian king, Amenhotep IV. During the reign of his father, there already had been written some noble ideas of God. In a sun hymn, Ra is said to be the guide over all peoples and all lands. No longer does the king believe that Ra is only the god of the Egyptians. Ra seems to be the god of all people. The hymn says that Ra is:

> Creator of all and giver of their sustenance. . . .
> Every land is in rejoicing
> At his rising everyday, in order to praise him.

THE REFORMS OF AMENHOTEP IV (IKHNATON)

When Amenhotep IV (Ikhnaton) succeeded his father as king (thirteen hundred and seventy-five years before Jesus was born) he began to make changes in the religion and to do away with the worship of many gods. This king said that there was one god and he called him by the name Aton. Not only did he use a new name for Ra, but he used a new symbol. Instead of the old symbols of a pyramid or a bird, the king used a sun disk with many rays and each ray ending in a human hand.

Because he was so earnest about his religion the king, Amenhotep IV, even changed his own name to "Ikhnaton," which means "Aton is satisfied." Then he sent forth men to change the names of other gods on public buildings and tombs to the name of the one god Aton.

Ikhnaton found that people in the ancient and wonderful capital of Thebes had so many memories of their old gods, that he built a new capital nearer to the sea at a place called

Amarna. Here he founded a city in honor of Aton, the one god of all people. He built a beautiful temple in Amarna, as well as temples in other parts of Egypt, to honor Aton.

Ra, the sun-god became one of the greatest gods of Egypt.

IKHNATON FAVORS PEACE

Ikhnaton was one of the first great peacemakers. Since Aton was the god of all people, the king did not expect him to be a war-god. When people today go to war they often forget this. They sometimes pray as if God were not interested in their enemies. Probably some of the nobles in Egypt did not like Ikhnaton because he would not go out with armies and chariots and horses to gain more land and to conquer other countries for Egypt. But the noble religion of this great king made him faithful to ways of justice and goodness. So we are not surprised to learn that Ikhnaton preferred the ways of peace.

IKHNATON'S IDEAS OF ATON

Ikhnaton's ideas of his god, Aton, have become known to us from pieces of a royal hymn which were found in the cemetery at Amarna. It is said that the king composed these lines to Aton:

Thou risest beautifully, O living Aton,
    Lord of Eternity;
Thou art glittering, beautiful, strong;
Thy love is great and mighty.
Thy rays furnish vision to every one of thy creatures,
Thy glowing hue brings life to the hearts of men,
When thou has filled the Two Lands with *thy love*.

Maker of every land,
Creator of that which is upon it;
Even men, all herds of cattle and the antelopes,
All trees that grow in the soil,
They live when thou dawnest for them,
Thou art the *mother* and the *father* of all that thou hast made.
As for their eyes, when thou dawnest,
They see by means of thee,
Thy rays illuminate the whole earth,
And every heart rejoices because of seeing thee,
When thou dawnest as their lord.

Thou hast made the distant sky to rise therein,
In order to behold all that thou didst make,
While thou wast yet alone,

All flowers live and what grows in the soil
Is made to grow because thou dawnest.[1]

In this ancient hymn, there is the idea that one God brought forth all races of men and gave them different speech and different colored skin. Aton gives life continuously. He provides light and heat for all his creatures. This god is like a

[1] Breasted, James H., *The Dawn of Conscience*, pp. 287, 288, 289.

father and a mother in his kindness and love for all people everywhere.[2]

HOME LIFE OF IKHNATON

Ikhnaton's religion made him a gentle and kind father. A little statue, found at Amarna, shows the king seated, holding his little daughter, the princess, on his knee and kissing her just as any kind father today might do.

Ikhnaton or Amenhotep IV worshiped one god.

Probably you have already read about and seen pictures of the Egyptian king Tutenkhamon. He became the son-in-law of Ikhnaton when he married one of his daughters. A lovely chair which came from the palace at Amarna was found in Tutenkhamon's tomb. On this chair is a scene showing the king resting, while his lovely queen stands before him with a jar of perfume from which she is gently touching her husband's clothing with fragrance. Many kings had been stern and formal. Ikhnaton seems to have brought friendliness and love into the palace at Amarna.

[2] Jesus referred to God as a father.

HYMNS OF ATON REMIND US OF THE PSALMS

There have been preserved parts of some other hymns giving praise to the god, Aton. These hymns were found on the tombs of some of the friends of Ikhnaton. Lines in these hymns remind us of Psalm 104 in our Bible.

Nofretete, Queen of Ikhnaton [1375-1358 B.C.].

Aton Hymn

How manifold are thy works!
They are hidden before men
O sole God, beside whom there is no other,
Thou didst create the earth according to thy heart;

Thou settest every man into his place
Thou suppliest their necessities,
Everyone has his food,
And his days are reckoned.
The tongues are divers in speech,
Their forms likewise and their skins are distinguished,
For thou makest different the strangers.

Thy rays nourish every garden;
When thou risest they live,
They grow by thee.
Thou makest the seasons
In order to make develop all thou hast made.
Winter to bring them coolness,
And heat that they may taste thee.[3]

IMPORTANCE OF THE CHARACTER, NOT THE NAME, OF THE GOD

Probably it was hundreds of years after the time of Ikhnaton before the Hebrews gave up their beliefs in many spirit gods and came to realize that there is one God in all of life. The name of the god is not so important as the ideas which people have about him. The Egyptians in the time of Ikhnaton used the name Aton for this one God. Much later, when there were some great Hebrew prophets who believed that there is one God, they probably called him Yahweh. Then finally the word for God became too holy for the Hebrews to speak of by name.

It is important to remember that all people do not agree about religious ideas. When the Jewish leaders after the exile said that there is but one God, most likely not all the Jews agreed with them. In ancient Egypt Ikhnaton was opposed by many Egyptians when he taught them to worship one god. Ikhnaton changed the names of the varied gods in all the great temples and on the pyramids to the one name, Aton. But when this great king died and his son-in-law Tutenkhamon,[4] a weaker king, came to the throne, noblemen and priests began to destroy the work of Ikhnaton and to return to the worship

[3] Breasted, James H., *The Dawn of Conscience*, pp. 284, 285.
[4] See pictures of his tomb in the *National Geographic Magazine*, May, 1923.

of their old gods. Ikhnaton's enemies took pleasure in destroying his teachings and in closing the beautiful temple of Aton in Amarna.

THE INFLUENCE OF IKHNATON'S BELIEFS

But even though much of the worship of Aton was destroyed, intelligent people had learned nobler things about God and we find these ideas being sung to their old god, Amon. A hymn to Amon reminds us of the hymn to Aton.

> Lord of truth, father of gods,
> Maker of men and creator of animals,
> Lord of that which is,
>
> .   .   .   .   .   .
>
> Lord of sweetness, great in love,
> At whose coming the people live.[5]

Another hymn addressed to Osiris says that he is the father and mother of men. This was also a part of the Aton belief. Here is a prayer to Ra which shows that the Egyptians' ideas of God were continuing to grow and to become very noble.

> Thou art the sole god, there is no other,
> Even Ra, who dawneth in the sky,
>
> .   .   .   .   .   .
>
> Who heareth the prayers of him who calls him,
>
> .   .   .   .   .   .
>
> Who maketh the people and the birds to live,
> Who supplieth the needs of the mice in their holes,
> The worms and the insects likewise.[6]

A poem of praise to Amon has been found in an old chapel in Thebes:

> Thou, O Amon, art the lord of the silent,
> Who cometh at the cry of the poor,
> When I cry to thee in my affliction,
> Then thou comest and savest me.
>
> .   .   .   .   .   .

[5] Breasted, James H., *The Dawn of Conscience*, pp. 310, 311.
[6] *Ibid.*, p. 313.

> When men cry unto thee,
> Thou art he that cometh from afar.[7]

About one thousand years before Jesus and long before the Hebrews had come to the realization of one God of all people and of a God of goodness, we find some Egyptians teaching very noble ideas of their Amon-Ra god. Here is some advice given by an official of Egypt to his son in those far-off days.

> Be not greedy for a cubit of land,
> And trespass not on the boundary of the widow. . . .
>
> .   .   .   .
>
> Plow the fields that thou mayest find thy needs,
> And receive thy bread from thine own threshing floor,
> Better is a bushel which God giveth to thee,
> Than five thousand gained by transgression.
> Better is poverty in the hand of God
> Than riches in the storehouse;
> And better are loaves when the heart is joyous,
> Than riches in unhappiness.
>
> .   .   .   .   .   .
>
> Of what advantage are fine clothes,
> When one is a transgressor before God?
> Take not gifts from the strong,
> Neither shalt thou oppress for him the weak,
> Justice is a great gift of God.[8]

Something to Do

1. If you are making a classbook on Egypt, try to discover more material for it in this chapter.
2. Make a list of things about Ikhnaton that seem to you to be very advanced for people living more than three thousand years ago.
3. When people come to think that God is a God of all people, why is it necessary for them to believe in peace, co-operation, and brotherhood? Read what Jesus gave as the two greatest religious teachings. See Mark 12:28-31.

---

[7] *Ibid.*, pp. 310, 311, 315. Compare some of these lines with Jesus' teachings in Matthew 6:28-30.
[8] *Ibid.*, pp. 322-324.

CHAPTER VII: THE HEBREWS LEARN FROM THE EGYPTIANS

The more we know about the religion of other people, the more we understand that all of them have been finding out something that was true about God. We have seen the beautiful teachings of Ikhnaton. We have noticed the progress made by later Egyptians in their ideas of God. Such religion in Egypt had taken thousands of years to develop. This was long before the Hebrews became a nation in Canaan.

The Hebrews must have had many ways of learning from them because Egypt often ruled over Canaan while the Canaanites lived there. Scholars believe that there were Hebrew tribes in Canaan for a very long time. Some of the Hebrews lived in Egypt for awhile. Today, scholars have dug up from ancient ruins many things that show that the inhabitants of Palestine borrowed from the Egyptians. In the Hebrew palace of king Ahab at Samaria have been found many carvings with Egyptian gods on them. Many other discoveries have been made which show that the Hebrews learned from the Egyptians.

The oldest written reference to the Hebrews was discovered in 1887 on some clay tablets buried in the sand at Amarna in Egypt. These tablets were letters written in the Babylonian language by kings of Palestine to the kings of Egypt. Among these clay tablet letters were some that were written about fourteen hundred years before the birth of Jesus. They tell about groups of nomads drifting into Palestine which was then under Egyptian rule. These nomads seemed to be entering the military service of Palestine. In Egypt no other reference to these ancient Hebrews has been found until about 1200 B.C. On an Egyptian monument set up by the ruler, Merneptah at

Thebes (Luxor), there is a hymn which boasts of a victory over the Hebrews.

> Israel is wasted, his seed is not.

In these days, the Hebrews were worshiping the ēlim in the desert or the baalim if they lived in Canaan. They had not reached the noble ideas of God which they later gave to the world and which Jesus believed and taught. Because they were a wandering people, they probably did not have any writings. It was about 850 B.C. when they were settled in Canaan that they were advanced enough to do any important writing. After this we are able to learn more about their beliefs.[1]

THE STORY OF JOSEPH

One of the loveliest stories told by the Hebrews is the one about Joseph. You may read it in the Bible in Genesis 37-48 as it was told by the Hebrews for thousands of years.

A Hebrew shepherd boy, Joseph, was sold by his jealous brothers to a passing caravan. Afterwards the guilty boys told their sorrowful father that Joseph had been killed by a wild animal. In the meantime Joseph was sold by the caravan to some Egyptians. Here he was tempted in many ways but he remained such a trustworthy person that the Egyptians gave him work to do. Then during a famine he was made director over the granaries and became one of the most powerful officials in Egypt.

At this same time Canaan was also suffering from famine, so it happened that Joseph's own brothers came to Egypt in search of grain. Joseph recognized them and had a good chance to test their ways. When he found that they were no longer so cruel as they had been to him as a boy, he revealed himself to them, forgave them for their bad treatment of him, and gave them plenty of grain to help them through the days of famine.

It seems very curious to learn that the Egyptians told a

[1] See Chapters XXIV and XXV about Hebrew writing.

story which is similar in some ways to the Joseph story in our Bible. For thousands of years this old story was repeated in various forms.

In Egypt it is known as the "Tale of the Two Brothers." Anubis and Bata were two gods who appeared as two peasant brothers. Bata is tempted by the wife of Anubis to be unfaithful to his brother, much as Joseph was tempted by the wife of an Egyptian officer. Bata arose in great anger and said to her, "Lo, thou art with me like a mother and thy husband is with me like a father, for he being older than I hath brought me up. What is this shameful thing that thou hast said to me?" Bata rushed forth into the field. The wife of Anubis became so angry because she had not succeeded in tempting Bata, that she told a false story to her husband. Believing her, Anubis took a weapon and hid himself near the stable door. Just as Bata came near with the cows from the pasture, two of them warned him of his danger and Bata fled away and was saved.

SOME TEACHINGS OF THE HEBREWS AND OF THE EGYPTIANS COMPARED

Perhaps you will be able to see that the Hebrew writings which are not so old as the Egyptians are much like them.

Egyptian	Hebrew
How manifold are thy works! They are hidden before men O sole God, beside whom there is no other. Thou didst create the earth according to thy heart.[2] More acceptable is the virtue of the upright man than the ox of him that doeth iniquity.[3]	O Lord, how manifold are thy works. In wisdom hast thou made them all: The earth is full of thy riches. (Psalms 104:24) To do righteousness and justice is more acceptable to Yahweh than sacrifice. (Proverbs 21:3)
The Egyptians came to think	Hundreds of years later the

[2] Breasted, James H., *The Dawn of Conscience*, p. 284.
[3] *Ibid.*, p. 156.

that their sun-god was a god of goodness.

Hebrews came to think that Yahweh was a god of love. Jesus was a great teacher of this idea.

An Egyptian wise man, called Amenemope, wrote some beautiful teachings for his son (about 1100 B.C.). He warns his son against cheating, being greedy, and seeking for riches. Honesty and goodness in every way seem to Amenemope to be the will of his god. His teachings are now preserved in the British Museum in London on a papyrus (Egyptian paper made from reeds). His words remind us of some of the wisest prophets and teachers of the later Hebrews and sometimes of Jesus. Parts of them were translated by the Hebrews and may be read in the Bible.[4]

> Of what advantage are fine clothes,
> When one is a transgressor before God?[5]
>
> . . . . . .
>
> If thou hearest good or evil,
> Leave it outside unheard,
> Put the good report on thy tongue,
> While the evil remaineth concealed. . . .[5]

Egyptian	Hebrew
Say not, "I have found a protector,	Say not thou, "I will recompense evil."
Now I can attack the hated man. . . ."	Wait for Yahweh, and he will save thee. (Proverbs 20:22)
Set thyself in the arms of God,	
Until thy silence overthroweth them (his enemies).[6] (Amenemope XXII, 1-8)	
Better is praise as one whom men love,	Better is a dry morsel and quietness therewith,
Than riches in the storehouse.[7] (Amenemope XVI, 11-12)	Than an house full of feasting with strife. (Proverbs 17:1)

---

[4] Proverbs 22:17-23:11, is largely drawn verbatim from the wisdom of Amenemope.
[5] Breasted, James H., *The Dawn of Conscience,* pp. 323, 325.
[6] *Ibid.,* p. 376.
[7] *Ibid.,* p. 375.

Egyptian	Hebrew
Weary not thyself to seek for more,	Weary not thyself to be rich.
When thy need is (already) secure.	. . . . .
If riches be brought to thee by robbery,	. . . . .
They will not abide the night with thee.	. . . . .
. . . . .	. . . . .
They have made themselves wings like geese,	For riches certainly make themselves wings
And they have flown to heaven.[8] (Amenemope IX, 14-X, 5)	Like an eagle that flieth toward heaven. (Proverbs 23:4, 5)

Something to Do

1. Continue making your book on Egypt.
2. Read aloud with a group in your class some of the Egyptian writings in this chapter. Try to learn them so that you may repeat them in perfect unison. Another group in the class may read together the Hebrew writings. Sometime you may use this verse speaking in a worship service to show what we owe to people of the past.
3. Plan to make a play out of the story of Joseph. Decide upon a few important scenes and then work out the speeches for each.

[8] *Ibid.*, p. 374.

CHAPTER VIII: THE HEBREWS BEGIN TO WORSHIP THE GOD, YAHWEH

In some Bibles, you will find Jehovah is the name used for one of the gods of the Hebrews. Scholars tell us that the correct name of this god was Yahweh.

The Hebrews probably did not always know or worship Yahweh because they were like other Semites in those far-off times. We have noticed that they worshiped spirits or ēlim in springs, trees, and stones. At first, the Hebrews had the very rude and barbarous habits of the other desert people. They even carried out the half-savage practice of slaying their first-born children, as a sacrifice to the tribal god.

Already we have noticed that each spirit or god in the desert was called an ēl. This word is found in our Bible connected with some of the old Hebrew names like Isra-el and Michael, which means "who is like ēl." Farther north in the country of Canaan, the gods had the name ba'al or lord. When some of the Hebrews settled in Canaan they also worshiped these baalim.

SOME HEBREWS LIVE IN EGYPT

At one time in their wanderings a few of the Hebrews took refuge in or near the land of Egypt because of their need of food in a time of severe famine. The Nile River, which ran through the center of Egypt, gave an unfailing supply of water to the people. It was used to water the fields, and the farmers raised plenty of grains and vegetables. Since Egypt was a rich country, and desert tribes often threatened invasion, a large wall was built across the eastern side of the country. It was called "The Wall of Egypt." Between the wall and the river Nile was "the land of Goshen." The soil was poor and only a

53

few Egyptians lived here. Nomads, like the Hebrews, who sought refuge here, could live as they always had in the desert. They tended their flocks, lived in tents, worshiped the ēlim and followed their old customs. According to ancient legends, the Egyptians began to treat the Hebrews as slaves and compelled them to help in building some of the great granaries of Egypt. Probably they had increased in numbers so much that the Egyptians were afraid that they would be dangerous in times of war. Life grew very hard for the Hebrews. Old Hebrew writings in our Bible tell us that their taskmasters often were cruel to them. They tried to force them to make sun-dried bricks without straw. Even to this day you may see people in Egypt mixing mud with straw and cutting it into little cakes and letting the sun bake it. If they do not have the straw, the bricks crumble and the work is lost.

An old city named Pithom has been found under the sand in Egypt. It had some houses built partly of bricks with straw and partly of bricks without straw. Perhaps this is one of the cities that the enslaved Hebrews had to build as a store city for Pharaoh. (See Exodus 1:11 in your Bible.)

These hard-driven Hebrews were eager to leave the land of Egypt. Perhaps they longed to join the other Hebrew tribes that lived in Canaan. Though their condition grew steadily worse, they did not easily find a way to escape.[1]

Moses seems to have been one of these Hebrews who lived in Egypt. His name comes from the Egyptian word "mose" meaning "child." The Bible contains many stories about him. Most of these stories were told for hundreds of years before they were written down. So we do not know exactly what Moses did do. We read that he was learned "in all the wisdom of the Egyptians," and that the Hebrews have always thought of him as

[1] For many years scholars have fixed the date of the Hebrew escape in the reign of Rameses II, sometime between 1295 and 1229 B.C. Dr. John Garstang places the fall of Jericho at about 1407 B.C. and the Hebrew escape from Egypt at about 1447 B.C. This would be in the reign of Amenhotep II. Probably the invasion and conquest of Canaan by the Hebrews took several hundred years.

one of their greatest leaders. In some way he was able to free them from their terrible bondage and to help them to make a new beginning in the desert.

MOSES FLEES TO MIDIAN

Moses saw his people suffering as slaves and harshly treated by their taskmasters in Egypt. One day he killed an Egyptian who was striking a Hebrew, and so it became necessary for him to flee from the country (Exodus 3:11, 12).

He found a place of refuge in the wilderness and made friends with a desert tribe of people known as Kenites or Midianites. Jethro, who was one of their religious leaders, became the special friend of Moses and gave him his daughter to marry. It was the custom of nomads, when the man was too poor to pay a dowry for his wife, to take him into the house of the girl and give him her name. So Moses lived according to his wife's customs and worshiped her gods.

Yahweh seems to have been a god of the mountain at Sinai.

MOSES LEARNS ABOUT YAHWEH

Among the gods of these Midianites, there was one which was regarded with special favor. This god was probably Yahweh. Some scholars think that Moses learned about him from Jethro and the other Kenites and so began to worship him also. We must remember that it was then thought very necessary to have the favor of the gods of the land in which one lived. One of the old stories handed down of Moses discovering Yahweh, makes it appear that Yahweh was a new god to him (Exodus 3:13, 14).

OTHER HEBREWS JOIN MOSES IN MIDIAN

When other Hebrews escaped from Egypt and joined Moses in the land of the Midianites, probably they also were introduced to Yahweh. Jethro, the priest of Midian and the father-in-law of Moses, arranged a great festival of sacrifice. On this occasion the Hebrews may have been initiated into the worship of the new god.

And Jethro, Moses' father-in-law, took a burnt offering and sacrifices for God (Yahweh); and Aaron came and all the elders of Israel, to eat the bread with Moses' father-in-law before God (Yahweh) (Exodus 18:12).

After this event Moses, Aaron, and seventy other Hebrew leaders, held a sacrificial feast to Yahweh without Jethro. They set up an altar near the mountain and arranged twelve pillars around it. Then animals were slain and their blood put in basins. Half of the blood was sprinkled on the altar. After this the Hebrews said, "All that Yahweh hath spoken will we do, and be obedient" (Exodus 24:7). Then Moses sprinkled the other half of the blood of the animals on the people to complete the pledge of loyalty to him.

Probably the people in the north of Arabia had known Yahweh for hundreds of years. During the very ancient times when Moses and the Hebrews worshiped this god, it was believed that Yahweh gave life to the tribe, and did many marvelous things. He gave sons and daughters. It was he who caused grass and trees to grow.

YAHWEH, A GOD OF THE VOLCANO

Yahweh may have been the god of the volcano in that country. Since there were no scientists to explain this terrible volcano spouting fire and smoke, it would not be surprising if the Midianites thought that it was a god who made it give forth the terrible thunderings and lightnings. The Bible speaks several times of Yahweh at a place called Sinai which was situated in the territory of the Kenites or Midianites. On this mountain Yahweh seemed to dwell. The sound of the volcano probably meant that Yahweh was speaking to his people. He seemed to appear when they saw fire on Sinai. Yahweh was worshiped with great fear. He seems to have been the most powerful god in their land, for he was able to send fire and destruction that made even the strongest helpless. The descriptions of Sinai in our Bible make it appear much like a volcano.

And Mount Sinai, the whole of it smoked, because Yahweh descended upon it in fire; and the smoke thereof ascended as the smoke of a furnace, and the whole mount quaked greatly. (Exodus 19:18)

Quite naturally all Semitic tribes believed that such strange happenings were caused by a god.

Then the earth shook and trembled,
The foundations also of the mountain quaked
And were shaken, because he was angry,
There went up a smoke out of his nostrils,
And fire out of his mouth devoured: (Psalm 18:7, 8)
The earth trembled, the heavens also dropped,
Yea, the clouds dropped water,
The mountains quaked at the presence of Yahweh,
Even yon Sinai at the presence of Yahweh, the God of Israel.
(Judges 5:4, 5)

When the Hebrews journeyed in the desert they referred in their old histories to the appearance of Yahweh guiding hem as "a pillar of fire" or "a pillar of cloud." Perhaps these were the fire and smoke of the great volcano.

YAHWEH, A GOD OF THE STORMS

The lightning and the rain were thought to be sent by Yahweh. Job says it is he who causes rain in the wilderness and the dry land (Job 38:25-27). In an old Psalm we read of the thunder as the voice of Yahweh (Psalm 29:3-9). Today we do not think as the Semites did about God. We have come to understand the causes of rain and storms and we feel that God works through orderly processes. Yet the ways of nature are still mysterious and wonderful to us and lead us to the belief that God is much greater that these Semitic people had ever imagined.

YAHWEH, A GOD OF WAR

Besides helping in the activities of nature, Yahweh was thought to be a god who helped his people in their wars. When the Kenite-Midianites won a victory in a time of war over some other tribe, they said that Yahweh had helped them defeat the god of the other tribe. In a way, wars were battles between the gods of different tribes. Since the Kenite-Midianites were often victorious, this must have made Yahweh a god to be feared and worshiped by other tribes. Perhaps this belief in Yahweh's power attracted Moses and the oppressed Hebrews. They needed a strong god. In one of the old Hebrew hymns it says: "Yahweh is a man of war" (Exodus 15:3). In many places in the Old Testament, we find that the Hebrews gave Yahweh the title "Yahweh Sebhaoth" which means that he is warlike.

EXPLANATIONS OF THE HEBREW ESCAPE FROM EGYPT

Several stories are given in the Bible about the escape of the Hebrews from their slavery and oppression in Egypt and of the way Yahweh helped them. In one group of stories (Exodus 5 to 12:29-38) Moses is described as using magical powers given him by Yahweh. Through these powers he was able to send disease and plagues upon the Egyptians. In these stories it appears that Yahweh was not interested in the Egyptians and sent many kinds of plagues and afflictions upon them in order to help the Hebrews to escape. Due to so much suffering and trouble, the ruler of Egypt finally gave the Hebrews permission to go. But after they had started, the king changed his mind and ordered his chariots to pursue them and bring them back. The story says an east wind, that blew all night, drove back the shallow water of the Sea of Sedge so that the Hebrews crossed the stream in safety. The Egyptians followed closely, but the waters began to return and many Egyptian soldiers and their horses were drowned (Ex. 14:28). Perhaps because the land was marshy and the heavy armour, chariots, and war horses of the Egyptians sank in the mud, and they were unable to cross the waters.

We do not know what really did happen. It was so very long ago, and the Hebrews had not yet learned to write down their history. Perhaps there was an earthquake and the eruption of a volcano. Something very unusual may have taken place. Whatever it was that happened, their escape convinced Moses that the volcano god, Yahweh, was the Hebrews' friend and deliverer. It was Yahweh now, not the ēlim, upon whom they should depend. So they promised always to worship him. We can understand how much these people must have been impressed by the wonders of a volcano and particularly by their escape from Egypt and from their oppressors. This escape from the Egyptians became so important that Jews tell the story to this day during their Passover festival.

Long after their thrilling escape, the Hebrews continued to sing praises to Yahweh. Some of these songs seem cruel and revengeful to us today. But wars have always made people savage and cruel. In these old songs Yahweh seems to be caring only for the Hebrews and not for the Egyptians. It was hundreds of years later before the Hebrews came to understand that there is a God of all people and that He loves them all equally well and that He is a God of love and of goodness.

Below are some lines of rejoicing which the Hebrews sang for many hundreds of years as they looked back upon their escape from Egypt:

I will sing to Yahweh for He has triumphed gloriously,
The horse and its rider has he thrown into the sea.
Yahweh is my strength and song,
For to me hath he brought deliverance;
This is my God, him I praise,
My fathers' God, him I extol.
Yahweh is a *man of war*,
Yahweh is his name.
The chariots of Pharaoh and his host hath he cast into the sea;
And the best of his captains have sunk down in the Red Sea.

Thy right hand, O Yahweh, is glorious in power,
Thy right hand, O Yahweh, dasheth in pieces the enemy. (Exodus 15:1-6)

Through the leadership of Moses, who had become a worshiper of Yahweh, the other Hebrews adopted this new god. Yahweh probably seemed much greater to them than the ēlim which were worshiped in the desert. Such desert spirits had no names. The new god had a name and this god became the chief Hebrew god. In later times, the great writers of the Hebrew religion could not think of a time when their people had worshiped many gods and spirits. They sometimes wrote as if Yahweh had always been their god. But we must remember that it took a great many hundreds of years for these people of the desert to grow in their understanding of life and of God before they could know that there is one God of love who is like a Father to His people everywhere.

When the Hebrews first worshiped Yahweh, he seems to us very cruel and warlike. Then after a few hundred years they began to think of Yahweh as requiring goodness and noble living instead of the offerings of animals and warlike deeds against their neighbors.

The Hebrews never forgot their wonderful escape from

Egypt and their great leader Moses. As the centuries passed by more and more of their great religious belief and laws were credited to Moses. Finally Moses seemed to the Hebrews to be the father and creator of all that was great in their history.

Chart I: The Religious Growth of the Hebrews

2000 B.C.	The Hebrews were wandering in the desert with their flocks. They worshiped the ēlim in rocks, trees and the oasis. At times some of the Hebrew tribes entered Canaan to find better living.
1400-1200 B.C.	After one of the Hebrew tribes had been in Egypt for a long time, they were led by Moses to escape. In the land of Midian they probably learned of the volcano god, Yahweh. After a long time of living as nomads this Hebrew tribe entered Canaan.
1040 B.C.	The Hebrews became victorious against the Philistines. Saul became their first king. They began to worship at high places and to adopt the festivals of the Canaanites. They brought Yahweh to their battles in arks. They also worshiped the baalim of the Canaanites.
967 B.C.	King Solomon built a temple in Jerusalem for Yahweh. Most of the Hebrews worshiped the baalim at the high places of the Canaanites.
750 B.C.	Some prophets of the Hebrews commenced to think of Yahweh as the ba'al of the Hebrews. Yahweh began to take the place of the other baalim of Canaan. He became the god of the weather, of crops, and of the land.
621 B.C.	A writer called "D" wrote a code of laws found in Deuteronomy which urges the destruction of all the old Canaanitish places of worship. It says that Jerusalem is the only place for the worship of Yahweh.
586 B.C.	Jerusalem was destroyed and the Hebrew leaders were carried away to Babylon. While in captivity these Jews, as they became known, grew and changed in their religious thinking.

They began to feel that there is one God of all

The Religious Growth of the Hebrews—Continued

people. They came to see that He requires justice and goodness rather than sacrifices of grain, animals, or children. Without a temple the Jews began to build synagogues in which to study about God.

A.D. Jesus came and taught some of the noblest things in our religion about God to his disciples. He also lived them out in his own life.

Something to Do

1. Read the imaginary letters of Benjamin in Chapter IX.

2. One of the oldest Hebrew writers, called "J" because he referred to the god of the Hebrews as Yahweh, says that this god became known to the Hebrews after their escape from Egypt. The discovery of Yahweh represents a new step in the growth of the Hebrew religion. Perhaps your class would like to tell the story of some of the changes in the Hebrew religion, beginning in the desert and continuing up to the time of Jesus, by means of a pageant. Scenes for different periods could be planned and an interlocutor or reader could read from a scroll the explanations of each tableau or pantomime. Religious customs in the desert may be found in Chapters I to IV. Chapter XVIII gives a glimpse of another period.

3. Add to the class poster any new ideas about God which you find in this chapter.

4. Perhaps you may wish to read some old stories about Moses' magical powers which must have been told around the camp fire for hundreds of years. They may be found in Exodus 5, 7, 8, 9, 10, 11, 12:29-38. What ideas of Yahweh do you discover in them? Contrast this early Hebrew idea of God with that of Jesus, hundreds of years later, as found in Luke 6:27-35; John 13:34; John 4:24, and I John 4:12, 16, 18.

CHAPTER IX: LETTERS FROM A BOY IN THE DESERT

If a boy in the time of Moses could have written a letter perhaps these are some things he would have told.

My dear Jacob:

I am very glad that we at last are away from the cruel Egyptians, but it has been a hard journey. The road was guarded by the Egyptians with their chariots, and we had to climb hills and go over great rocks in order to escape. Getting away from the Egyptians was the most exciting adventure I have ever had. When they pursued us in their chariots we thought that escape was impossible. We were very much frightened. But Moses told us that Yahweh was on our side. Suddenly a very wonderful thing happened! The earth shook and the wind began to blow and the water moved like a small tide at sea. All of us hurried across the shallow place caused by the wind at the narrowest place in the sea. As we looked backward, we saw that the water was moving back again and that many of the Egyptians' chariots and horses could no longer follow us. At last we were safe! We felt certain that it was the god, Yahweh, that had saved us.

After a long journey during the night and most of the next day, we became very tired. The sun was scorching hot, but we could not stop. I was ever so thirsty, but my mother said that I must wait for a drink of water until the end of the day's journey.

Before we had our supper the women put up the large black tents. I helped to drive the tent pegs and stretch the ropes. Other boys unloaded the donkeys and camels. Some had to milk the goats. How hungry and thirsty everyone was that first night! There was so little water and food that each one could have only a tiny sip and some curds and cheese. Then we began to wish that we were back in Egypt, where there were melons, cucumbers, rice, meat, dates, nuts, raisins, and water.

After the sun went down it became cool and we built a fire. Everyone talked about the wonderful escape from the Egyptians. Miriam, the sister of Moses, took a timbrel and began to dance. Then all the women took up their timbrels and began to dance and sing. Everyone was glad because we would not have to make bricks and be whipped by the cruel taskmasters of Egypt any more. After that I went into our tent, wrapped up in my goatskin rug, and went to sleep.

The next day Moses prepared a sacrifice. He offered a lamb as a burnt offering to show Yahweh, the god of Midian, how glad we were that he had saved us.

Then we traveled on and on over more hills and sand, while the hot sun beat down upon us. Everyone became very tired. I heard some people scolding because there was no water to drink.

On the following day the people complained even more. The babies cried and their mothers could not quiet them. Moses reminded us that Yahweh was with us and would take care of us. He tried to comfort the people and was very kind to everyone. He said he was certain that we should find water. Suddenly, after three days, one of the men saw something green. People became very excited! I ran as fast as I could. At last there was beautiful, clear water! I dropped down and drank eagerly. But I wished that I had waited. The beautiful, clear water was bitter! This made everyone very angry. They said to Moses, "What shall we drink?"

Then Moses looked up and saw a tree near the well. He took some branches and put them into the well, and soon the water was sweet and we drank all we wanted. This made our people very happy. The goats and cattle and camels were given water.

The people felt better and listened to Moses. He told them that we were to go towards the mountain called Sinai, where we should live for a while. So we started on our journey again, until we came to the oasis in the desert where we are now. Here there are twelve springs and many, many palm trees, and we are all very happy.

Now I must go and milk the goats, but I shall try to write again.

Your long-time-ago friend,

Benjamin.

BENJAMIN WRITES ANOTHER LETTER

My dear Jacob:

At last we have reached Mount Sinai about which Moses has told us so much. As we came near to it, I was frightened. There was a sound like the blowing of a mighty wind. Then there was a great storm of thunder and lightning and Mount Sinai became covered with black clouds and smoke. All the people in our camp trembled with fear. Moses says that the god, Yahweh, lives in the smoke of the mountain.

This god, we believe, is much stronger and greater than the gods in Egypt. He helped us to escape when we were fleeing from Egypt.

Moses called my father and all the older men together for a meeting. Once again he asked them to remember that Yahweh will be their special friend. Everyone was so thankful for all that he has done, that they united in promising: "All that Yahweh hath spoken we will do."

One day Moses went up into the mountain to worship Yahweh. There were terrible lightnings, rain came down in torrents, and the wind and the thunder grew louder and louder. While the people waited for Moses, they became more and more frightened. Many cried out in terror. Some wished that we had never left Egypt.

After several days, Moses came back to us and everyone was glad. He helps us to find food and water. Then there are tribes out here who get the dates and the pasture for their herds before we do. We get along much better when Moses is here to help us.

You know that we do not have any laws like we had in Egypt and everyone tries to do as he pleases. Moses spends much time trying to settle our quarrels. There have been so many that he has had to have some helpers and he deals only with the hardest cases. My father is one of his helpers and is busy all the time. There is trouble over the herds. Then there is stealing, bribery and borrowing. Moses and my father are helping people to obey some of the laws so that they can live more happily together.

As a pledge of our loyalty to Yahweh, Moses set up twelve tall stones and all the young men like my brother Dan, offered burnt offerings and peace offerings of oxen unto Yahweh. Moses caught all of the blood of the animals in a basin and sprinkled half of it on the pillars. The people then pledged themselves to be faithful to Yahweh. They said, "All that Yahweh hath spoken will we do and be obedient." After this promise Moses took the rest of the blood and sprinkled it on all the people. This means that we shall be friends with Yahweh. I am so glad because I believe that he is greater than the other gods whom we have served and we need his protection while we are in the land of Midian.

Your very long-time-ago friend,

Benjamin.

CHAPTER X: ARKS FOR THE GODS

Arks or boxes were used for the gods by many of the ancient peoples in the days of the early Hebrews. The Egyptians had a sacred ship for each god and the image of the god was borne in solemn procession up and down the Nile River. In Babylonia arks or boxes were likewise used to carry the images of the gods in the processions, which marched along the streets on great feast days.

THE ARKS OF THE HEBREWS

We have already noticed that the Semites considered it necessary to worship the gods of the land wherever they happened to be. When the Hebrews began to worship Yahweh, they carried their god in an ark, just as other people carried their gods.

Sacred boxes were well known to all the people in Palestine. The earliest story of the sacred box among the Hebrews begins during the time when they were struggling to settle in Canaan. This sacred box or ark was thought of as a little temple in which the spirit of the god came to help the priest decide important questions. It was not too large to be carried by one person. Probably a strap around the shoulders and neck helped to support it. (See I Kings 2:26, Judges 18:20, and I Samuel 2:28.)

While the priest carried the ark, an inquirer stood before it and asked questions of the deity. I Samuel 23:9-11 tells of David calling for a priest to bring the box. Then David asks Yahweh about the plans of Saul and the priest helps him to get an answer from the box. Answers were usually given by yes or no. I Samuel 14:19 shows that the priest put his hand inside the box and did something which after a time indicated an answer to the question asked.

After the Hebrews settled in Palestine, they continued to think of Yahweh speaking to them through the ark. Probably they had arks in many of their holy places (places of worship). A box or ark was also kept in the homes of wealthy people,

This is a pottery shrine or tiny temple and is probably much like the ancient arks. These small temples or arks were regarded by the Hebrews in Canaan as the dwelling place of a god or of Yahweh. The nomads probably used a tiny tent as a covering for sacred stones and as a house for the deity of the tribe.

who could afford to have their own priest. Judges 17:5 records a story of Micah who had such a chapel in his home.

THE ARK IN WAR TIMES

In the Bible most of the stories of the ark or box of Yahweh refer to its use in battles. A very old section of the Old Testament says that it went ahead of Moses and the Hebrews after their escape from Egypt, when they were marching (Numbers 10:33-36). During the wars of Saul and David, an ark was carried to battle and attended by a priest. One of the arks which was used to carry Yahweh into battle was said to have been taken from a place of worship at Shiloh.

For a great many years after the Hebrews left Sinai they carried Yahweh in the ark. Whenever they went to battle they carried it to show that Yahweh was with them. As it started out at the head of the army, these words were spoken:

> Rise up, Yahweh
> Let thine enemies be scattered
> And let them that hate Thee flee before thee.

When the ark came back from victory these words were uttered,

> Rest, O Yahweh,
> Thou myriads of regiments of Israel.

It was thought that Yahweh was the god of battle, worth more than many regiments of men. After he had brought victory he was returned to his tent for rest.

There are numerous curious stories about the ark in the Old Testament. One of them may be found in I Samuel 4:7. Here the Hebrews ascribe their defeat in battle to the capture of the ark by the Philistines. This was a terrible day for the Israelites. Four thousand of their men were killed in battle by their powerful enemies, the Philistines. After the people gathered into the camp, they said, "Wherefore hath Yahweh smitten us today before the Philistines? Let us fetch the ark of Yahweh, that it may come among us, and save us out of the hand of our enemies."

The Hebrews sent down to Shiloh for their ark. When the bearers arrived with it, there went up a great shout from the camp of Israel. The Philistines heard the noise of the shout and asked, "What meaneth the noise of this great shout in the camp of the Hebrews?"

In the midst of all their fright, a leader of the Philistines

cried out, "Have courage! Be men! Fight that you may not become slaves of the Hebrews as they have been slaves to you."

Then the Philistines rushed into battle and fought so sav-
agely that the Hebrews began to flee. Thousands were killed,
but even worse for the Hebrews, the ark of their god was
taken.

Probably a Philistine looked like this.

When news of the disaster reached the camp of the Hebrews, they cried out in despair. Eli, one of their aged leaders,
was so overcome that he fell from his seat and died.

The Philistines, with great rejoicing, brought the ark to
their town of Ashdod and placed it in the temple of their god,
Dagon.

In the morning when the Philistines came to their temple,
the Hebrew writer of the story humorously discredits the
god, Dagon, by telling that they found his image had fallen
down and broken into pieces. This ancient writer believed
that in the presence of the mightier god, Yahweh, Dagon had
fallen over and broken.

While the ark was in their midst, a disease began to spread over the land and when the men of Ashdod saw what was happening they said, "The ark of the god of Israel must not remain with us longer. This god is against us."

It was decided to send the ark to Gath, but on its arrival there, a pestilence began to spread in that town. Wherever the Philistines carried the ark, there was disease. Finally the leaders of the Philistines held a meeting and said, "Send the ark of god back to its own place. Do not let it stay among us and our people. The god of the Israelites is against us and the sorrow of our towns rises up to heaven."

So the Philistines prepared a new cart to carry the ark back to the Hebrews. They said: "We must not send the ark back empty," for they believed a special gift to the god of the Hebrews might win his favor and take away their diseases.

Beside the ark, in the new cart, they put a similar box containing golden images of mice and of tumors. These objects represented the troubles which it was believed the Yahweh god had brought upon them.

How could the Philistines be certain that Yahweh had caused these troubles? This is how they decided. They fastened two cows, which had never been yoked before, to the cart. If the cows took the straight road back to Israel, it was agreed that the god of the ark had caused their afflictions. If the cows chose another road, then it was merely an accident.

The leaders of the Philistines followed the cart and they probably chased the cows bearing the ark toward the land of Israel. The ark was taken safely back to the Hebrews while the Philistines returned home, glad to be freed from this Hebrew ba'al, to whom they ascribed all their troubles.

AN ARK PLACED IN THE HEBREW TEMPLE

More than two hundred years after the Hebrews had come to Palestine one of their kings named Solomon built a temple at Jerusalem for Yahweh to dwell in (I Kings 6:19). In the

Old Testament there is a long story about placing one of the arks in this temple of Solomon. (See I Kings 8.)

Long, long afterwards, Solomon's temple was destroyed. Then stories about arks began to be written down. Some of these stories we find in our Bible. But there is something very curious about them. They often read as if there had been but one ark. They say that this ark was used as the residence of Yahweh while leading the Hebrews in all their wanderings and in all their battles. In many of the Bible references these writers whom we call P and D claim that the ark was made especially to contain two sacred stones with ten laws given by Yahweh. Probably the idea of one ark began to grow in later times because the Hebrews were being taught that there was but one most holy place and that was in the temple of Jerusalem.

Bible scholars today know that there were many arks. The Hebrew word when translated means box. Few scholars really believe that the ark was used for these ten commandments because these laws seem to have been formed hundreds of years later, after the Hebrew religion had progressed a great deal more than it did in the desert.

THE HEBREWS CHANGE THEIR IDEAS ABOUT THE ARK

The superstition of consulting the box of Yahweh seems to have lasted for many centuries. Even after the Hebrews had been settled in Palestine several hundred years, we read of a great teacher called Jeremiah (about 626 B.C.) trying to persuade people in the north to go to their prophets in place of the arks. He says, " 'And it shall come to pass, when you increase and multiply in the land in those days,' declares Yahweh, 'that men will no longer speak of the box of Yahweh, nor will it enter their minds, nor will they invoke it, nor will they resort to it; neither will it be manufactured any more' " (Jeremiah 3:16). These words show that the Hebrews continued to consult the ark to find out Yahweh's wishes for hundreds of years after they had settled in Canaan.

Something to Do

1. What material do you find in this chapter for your pageant or pictures that will help to tell the story of the Hebrew quest for God?

2. Perhaps you would enjoy writing a play for your class showing the experiences of the Hebrews and the Philistines with the ark. Read the story in I Samuel 4:1-6;16. If possible you may wish to read in *The Pilgrim Elementary Teacher* for March, 1933, a play created by some young people.

3. Have you ever heard of Christians praying to God to help them win a war? Suppose several nations did this. How could a loving God answer such prayers? Is the God of Jesus a war-god? Read again I John 4:12, 16, 18.

4. Try to find out what the Quakers think about war. What does your church teach about war? Write down some good reasons for believing God is in favor of ways of love and brotherhood between nations.

5. Why would the ancient Hebrews and their neighbors believe in war-gods?

CHAPTER XI: WORSHIP IN THE NEW LAND OF CANAAN

After the Hebrew tribe had escaped from the land of Egypt the Hebrews continued in the nomadic ways of their fathers before them. They lived in tents much as the Arabs do today, and they depended upon their flocks for food. North of them lived the Canaanites in walled cities. Outside of the cities farmers plowed the land and raised grain and fruits. The Canaanites had been growing in their civilization for nearly a thousand years. While the Hebrews had been wandering in the desert, the Canaanites had been learning many things from the great countries of Babylonia and Egypt. Egypt had been invading this land of Canaan for about two thousand years before the Hebrews settled it. So it was only natural, as we have seen, that many of the Egyptian ideas should be well known to the people of Canaan.

Eagerly the Hebrews from Egypt hoped for the day when they also might live in this pleasant land of Canaan. But for a long time they were obliged to live in the desert south of Canaan. Probably their chief center was around the sacred spring at Kadesh. The Bible gives us many different stories about the Hebrews' trying to enter and to conquer this country to the north of them. Very often this warfare was cruel and terrible as war always is.

Since it was the custom to ask the help of the gods in times of war, the Hebrews depended upon their new Yahweh god to assist them in conquering the people of Canaan. (See Judges 1:19.) In these days the Hebrews believed that Yahweh was interested only in them. Probably this was because the Hebrews remembered their escape from the Egyptians and never ceased to sing praises to Yahweh who they said had delivered them from their enemies. In the new land he went before them in the ark and helped them. At first, when the Hebrews tried to take Canaan for themselves, they could not break down the strong walls of the cities so they were obliged to live in the rural parts of the land while the Canaanites occupied the cities. (See Joshua 17:12, 13.)

THE HEBREWS LEARN FROM THE CANAANITES

Gradually the Hebrews made friends with the Canaanites and married their sons and daughters. They slowly gave up the ways of their desert life and began to learn the more civilized ways of the Canaanites (Judges 1:27, 28).

During their desert wanderings the Hebrews had depended upon nature for food. In Canaan, it became necessary to learn how to cultivate the land and to raise their own food, just as the Canaanites did. As they watched the Canaanites hold great ceremonies for their baalim (gods of the land) during the times of planting the grain and reaping the harvest, the Hebrews quite naturally felt that they must do the same in order to be successful farmers.

The Canaanites believed that there were spirits or baalim in springs, trees, mountaintops, caves, and tombs. Wherever there was a spirit, the people built a wall around the spot and called it a "high place." Within the wall was set up a stone pillar which was called bēth-ēl, or "house of an ēl." At such places all over the land the Canaanites worshiped different spirits, and poured out the blood from their sacrifices.

The Hebrews also began to worship these gods of the land at the ancient altars of the Canaanites, just as had been done for hundreds of years by all who had lived in the country. Since no one believed that there was but one god, it seemed very important to keep the friendship of the gods in different places. At the same time the Hebrews remembered their god, Yahweh, and carried him to battle with them in the arks.

THE USE OF IMAGES

The Hebrews used images to aid them in their worship just as other people around them did. When Moses led the Hebrews in the worship of Yahweh, we read of him carrying a magic staff. Probably it was a serpent staff such as he had seen the Egyptians use. When people were ill Moses set up a shining image of a serpent. It seems that the Hebrews kept this kind of an image for their worship and had burned incense to it for hundreds of years. We read of King Hezekiah's removing it from the temple in Jerusalem several hundred years after the Hebrews had come to Palestine:

. . . he brake in pieces the brazen serpent that Moses had made; for unto those days the children of Israel did burn incense to it. (II Kings 18:4)

The Hebrews made a law which said, "Thou shalt make thee no molten gods" (Exodus 34:17). Probably this law merely

In Canaan Yahweh was sometimes worshiped in the image of a bull at the shrines of Dan and Bethel. [I Kings 12:26-29.]

forbade them to make expensive images of silver or gold. It did not forbid stone or wooden idols. We read in the Bible that David, one of the Hebrew kings, had an image called a teraph, which was so large that it was put in his bed when his enemies were seeking to kill him. It deceived them and David escaped (I Samuel 19:13-16).

Later on, some of the Hebrews made more expensive images of Yahweh. These were fashioned after those of the Canaanites and represented little bulls.

Some of the Hebrew leaders began to advance in their religion, especially after they were carried away to Babylonia as exiles. Gradually men called prophets began to condemn the use of images. Read the criticism of a writer who lived only a few hundred years before Jesus' time and you will see how slowly the masses of the Hebrews changed their ideas of God.

And now they sin more and more, and have made them molten images of their silver, even idols according to their own understanding, all of them the work of the craftsmen. (Hosea 13:2)

THE HEBREWS LEARN THE WAYS OF CITY PEOPLE

Jerusalem was a city built upon high hills and so for a long time the Hebrews were not able to capture it from the Canaanites (Judges 1:21). As time passed the Hebrews grew more and more powerful. They elected Saul, who was a military chieftain, to become their king. Later he was succeeded by King David. We read in the Bible that it was David who finally conquered the city of Jerusalem. So Jerusalem was sometimes called the city of David (II Samuel 5:7).

As the Hebrews settled in Canaan, they learned the ways of farming and of city life. They built houses instead of tents. Some city people became prosperous and wore rich clothing and enjoyed luxuries. Of course there were many Hebrews who continued to live in the country. These rural Hebrews despised city ways and said that they were sinful.

When Solomon followed his father David as king, he tried to imitate the rulers of countries around him. At Jerusalem he built for himself a beautiful palace, and another one for his Egyptian wife. He built fine stables for his horses. Scholars have found ruins of Solomon's buildings in other parts of

Palestine. These new luxuries became a burden to the Hebrews who had to pay the taxes for this government.

WORSHIP AT JERUSALEM

There was a very large rock on top of the mountain at Jerusalem. People came to it to thresh their grain. They also came here to worship and to offer sacrifices to some ba'al on this rock. No one knows for how many hundreds or thousands of years this had been done.

After Solomon had built his palaces in Jerusalem, he decided to build a small temple to Yahweh at this ancient altar of the Canaanites. As the years passed by the Hebrews began to think that Yahweh dwelt in this temple at Jerusalem. One writer says the god's "home-fires are within Jerusalem" (Isaiah 31:9).

About 621 B.C. parts of Deuteronomy were written.[1] It is a rewording of Exodus 20-23 but includes very great changes in worship. It urges the destruction of all the old shrines and places of worship. Jerusalem is made the chief center for Yahweh worship.[2]

YAHWEH BECOMES THE BA'AL OF THE HEBREWS

While the Hebrews worshiped the baalim of the Canaanites they also began to call Yahweh their ba'al. We find Gideon being given the name Jerrub-baal. Saul named his son Ish-baal while Jonathan named his son Meri-baal. Gradually the Hebrews began to think of Yahweh as the ba'al of the land. Agricultural festivals were now held for Yahweh rather than for Canaanitish baalim. After the Hebrews had lived in Palestine for several hundred years, some of their leaders told them that Yahweh did not wish to be called ba'al any longer (Hosea 2:16).

When Yahweh took the place of the other gods of Canaan

[1] Deuteronomy 5-26 and 28:1-46.
[2] Read Deuteronomy 7:5, 6, 25 and 8:18, 19.

all kinds of powers were ascribed to him. He became the creator of man and beast. He made earth and sky. The sun, moon, and stars obeyed his command. He appeared in storms, lightning, fire, earthquake, when he went forth to help the Hebrews.[3]

Chart II: Order of Some Events

About 2200 B.C.	Hammurabi created a famous code of laws in Babylonia.
Before 2200 B.C.	Hebrews lived as nomads in the desert and worshiped ēlim. Canaanites living in Palestine were growing in their civilization. They learned much from Babylonia and from Egypt.
About 1479 B.C.	Egypt began its conquest of Canaan.
About 1335 B.C.	Ikhnaton of Egypt worshiped one god, a god of all people, and believed in peace. Egyptian power over Canaan was weakened. The Canaanites, with their advanced civilization, occupied Canaan.
Between 1400 and 1200 B.C.	A tribe of Hebrews escaped from Egypt to which their ancestors had come during a famine. Moses acted as leader. They discovered a new god, Yahweh. These Hebrews finally entered Canaan. They captured Jericho. There was a long struggle before they were really settled in Canaan.
About 1040 B.C.	The Hebrews fought many battles against the Philistines, Saul acting as leader. Later he became the first king of the Hebrews in Palestine.
About 1010 B.C.	David, their second Hebrew king, began to rule over much of Palestine with Jerusalem as his capital.
About 967 B.C.	Solomon, the third Hebrew king, built a temple to Yahweh in Jerusalem.

Something to Do

1. What material do you find in this chapter for your pageant or your pictures?

[3] Judges 5:4; I Samuel 12:17; Psalm 18.

Turn to Chart I at the end of Chapter VIII and to Chart II at the end of this chapter in order to find out where some of the important changes in the Hebrew story took place.

2. What do you think the Hebrews learned from the Canaanites? How did they imitate the Canaanites in their religion?

3. What happened several hundred years later when the Hebrews declared Yahweh the ba'al of Palestine? Notice the new powers of Yahweh as revealed in the stories told by later Hebrew writers. Judges 5:4; I Samuel 12:17 and Psalm 18.

4. Compare the Yahweh known to the Hebrews about 1400 B.C. at Sinai with Yahweh in Palestine 621 B.C. See Deuteronomy 7:5, 6, 8, 10, 16, 25 and 8:18, 19. How does Yahweh wish the Hebrews to treat other nations? Read where Yahweh dwelt: I Kings 22:19; II Kings 7:2 and Genesis 19:24.

CHAPTER XII: YAHWEH BECOMES THE HEBREW GOD IN CANAAN

The experiences with the god Yahweh had been so impressive that the Hebrews were always filled with particular awe and reverence for this god. After their escape from Egypt, we remember that an ancient story tells that the Hebrews were so overjoyed that they pledged themselves to become his faithful and devoted worshipers.

Probably it was a long time after they had come to Canaan that a law was made demanding that the Hebrews worship Yahweh alone. This law says, "Thou shalt worship no other God." People had not yet come to realize that there is but one God. So this law probably meant that, though there were other gods, the Hebrews must give their loyalty and devotion to Yahweh alone.

After many, many years in Canaan we have noticed that some of the Hebrews began to think of Yahweh doing the things for which they had once worshiped the baalim of Canaan. In place of another ba'al, Yahweh was worshiped as the god of the weather and of the crops. Great harvest festivals were no longer celebrated in honor of the baalim of Canaan but in remembrance of Yahweh. Old customs and ways of celebrating the festivals of sowing and reaping remained much as they always had among the Canaanites, but the Hebrews gave them new meaning and changed them to the glory and honor of Yahweh.

The ancient Passover feast of the desert days continued to be celebrated as the birth time of animals. After a few hundred years in Palestine the Hebrews gradually came to observe the festival in honor of Yahweh. At the time of the gathering of the first of the barley crop, the first grain was offered to the

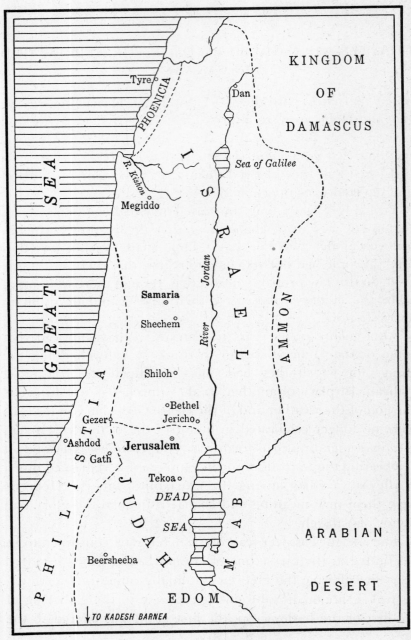

No. 2. Palestine Divided

deity, as a gift in the form of unleavened bread (Exodus 23:15 and 34:18).

Seven weeks later, they celebrated a new agricultural festival at the time of the ripening of the wheat (Exodus 23:16 and 34:22).

In the autumn, they had a festival of grape gathering, instead of the date festival of desert days. This third festival was a celebration of all of the harvest. These festivals gradually came to be connected with Yahweh as the god of life and growth (Judges 21:19).

On the occasion of such festivals, or feasts, the Hebrew men were expected to journey to one of the important national places of worship such as Shiloh, Bethel, Dan and Jerusalem (Exodus 23:17).

A PROPHET CRITICIZES THE KING

After Ahab became the Hebrew king, he married the princess Jezebel from the city of Tyre. They lived in luxury. As a great favor to his queen, Ahab built for her special places to worship her god Melkart (I Kings 16:31-33).

This displeased the more rural Hebrews, particularly Elijah. He was a man of the desert and believed strongly in desert ways. He talked of Yahweh as a stern god who despised the luxuries of the city people and their king, Ahab. When Elijah spoke he seemed to be giving a message for the Hebrew god, Yahweh. One ancient story says that he went boldly to the palace and condemned king Ahab for bringing in all this luxury, and especially for permitting the worship of the god Melkart.

A very ancient and interesting story of Elijah has been handed down to us in the Bible (I Kings 18:21-46). It shows that some of the Hebrews were beginning to think of Yahweh as the god of all of Palestine. Perhaps Elijah was one who helped this belief to spread among the Hebrews.

The story says that there was a terrible drought in the land

of Canaan. Farmers were anxious for rain. Probably the Hebrews and the Canaanites had tried to persuade the baalim of
the land to send rain. Elijah believed that Yahweh was the god
of rain. He wanted to prove this to the Hebrews, so he challenged the worshipers of ba'al Melkart to meet at Mount Car-
mel on the boundary line dividing the land of Yahweh and
the land of Melkart. In this way it came about that worshipers
of ba'al Melkart and of ba'al Yahweh gathered to make a sacrifice to prove which god could control the weather.

Elijah said, "If Yahweh be God, follow him; but if ba'al
then follow him." He ordered two animals to be slain and
placed on an altar on top of some wood without any fire. Then
he said, "Call ye on the name of your God, and I will call on
the name of Yahweh; and the god that answers by fire, let him
be God." So it was agreed.

First the ba'al Melkart worshipers prepared their offering.
Then they cried out to their ba'al to send fire. They did this for
half a day and no fire came. They cut themselves with knives.
They danced about the altar. But the story says there was no
answer.

After the worshipers of ba'al Melkart had tried in vain,
Elijah took his turn. He prepared the altar for Yahweh with
twelve pillars of stone. He even poured water over the offering
and on the wood. Then he prayed, "O Yahweh, the God of
Abraham, of Isaac, and of Israel, let it be known this day that
Thou art God in Israel."

The story says that after his prayer was finished, fire fell and
burned up the animal, and the wood, and the stones and all
the water. When the people saw this they fell on their faces
and cried out, "Yahweh, He is God; Yahweh, He is God!"

After Elijah had finished his sacrifice, he ordered the Hebrews to kill all the leaders who worshiped ba'al Melkart. The
story ends by saying that clouds began to gather over the
mountain, the wind came and there followed a great rain

which ended the drought. Elijah, of course, believed the drought had been sent by Yahweh to punish the Hebrews.

This ancient story was told by the Hebrews over and over again in the later days, when they had learned to think that Yahweh was the ba'al of Canaan. It was used as a sermon or lesson to these early people to prove to them that Yahweh alone was the Hebrew god of Canaan and that he only should be worshiped by them. The story shows to us today how much more the Hebrews at that time still had to learn before they could think of God as the God of all people and as a God of love. Ba'al worship was not destroyed by Elijah, for we read a few years later of the ruler, Jehu, inviting all worshipers of ba'al to their place of worship and then cruelly killing them.[1]

A PROPHET DENOUNCES THE WORSHIP AT BETHEL

Amos, the stern shepherd of Tekoa was one of the religious prophets who said that the Hebrews should worship only Yahweh alone. He had always lived out-of-doors on the hills near Jerusalem. He favored living as he believed the Hebrews had lived in the long past. He disliked the ways of city people and felt that all of their grand clothing and houses and parties were despised by the god Yahweh. More than this, he said that Yahweh was displeased with their offerings and religious cere- monies at the "high place" in Bethel.[2] This was the royal shrine and the center of all worship in the northern kingdom. King Jeroboam had set up a small golden bull to represent Yahweh, who had brought the Joseph tribe of the Hebrews out of Egypt (I Kings 12:28).

Let us imagine a scene in Bethel during a great religious feast, when Amos appeared in his rough peasant costume and began to condemn the Hebrews who had gathered to wor- ship Yahweh. In the following scene from Amos, someone

---

[1] II Kings 10:18, 19, 21, 23, 25, 28.

[2] Bethel must have been a very old city. Archaeologists have found houses of stone that were built about 1200 B.C. They had large rooms built around the sides of an inner court open to the sky.

may take the part of Amos and the priest, while another reads
the setting.[3]

TEACHER: While people were offering animals as sacrifices at
the great religious feast at Bethel, and priests and people
were becoming more and more noisy, Amos, a shepherd
prophet from Judah, suddenly began to speak.
AMOS: When the Eternal thunders loudly from Jerusalem,
then the pasture lands are woebegone, the ridge of Karmel
withers. (Amos 1:2)
THE PEOPLE: Let us find out what this man is saying.
TEACHER: The people drew nearer.
AMOS: The Eternal declares:
"After crime upon crime of Gaza
I will not relent,
for they would bear off a whole population
and sell them into slavery to Edom;" (Amos 1:6)
TEACHER: The people believed that the Philistines deserved
punishment.
AMOS: The Eternal declares:
"After crime upon crime of Edom
I will not relent:
for sword in hand he pursued his brother,
stifling all pity,
he held to his anger
and cherished his wrath." (Amos 1:11)
TEACHER: These words pleased the Hebrews. They were glad
to have enemies suffer. So the prophet went on to tell of
other countries that would be punished. By this time a
large crowd was listening to Amos. Then he said:
AMOS: The Eternal declares:
"After crime upon crime of Israel
I will not relent,
for they sell honest folk for money,
the needy for a pair of shoes." (Amos 2:6)

[3] The quotations of Amos are taken from the Moffatt translation of the Bible.

THE PEOPLE: This is amazing! Does he mean to say that Israel shall be punished for selling as slaves people who fail to pay their debts? What does this have to do with Yahweh? Do we not bring him rich gifts?

AMOS: So now I make your steps collapse,
as a cart collapses, laden with sheaves,
and flight shall fail the swift,
the sturdy shall not hold their own,
the warrior shall not escape alive. (Amos 2:13, 14)

TEACHER: So Amos warned the people that Assyria would come and destroy them.

AMOS: I strike down winter-house and summer-house together,
and ivoried houses perish—
ay, many a house is swept away:
by order of the Eternal. (Amos 3:15)

TEACHER: Certainly the people did not like these awful words. But Amos wanted them to change their ways, and he knew that the people who lived in beautiful and rich houses were those who were destroying the country and making the poor more miserable. Yet the people had so many religious feasts that they felt sure that Yahweh would favor them. Imagine how shocked they must have been when Amos said:

AMOS: Your sacred festivals? I hate them, scorn them;
Your sacrifices? I will not smell their smoke;
you offer me your gifts? I will not take them;
you offer fatted cattle? I will not look at them.
No, let justice well up like fresh water,
let honesty roll in full tide. (Amos 5:21-24)

TEACHER: Amos believed that justice and goodness were the things that Yahweh desired above everything else. Amos remembered desert ways of justice and these city people had forgotten them. He told the people that they would be punished. But they refused to listen to him. The priest at Bethel, Amaziah, sent word to Jeroboam, king of Israel.

AMAZIAH: Amos is conspiring against you in the very midst of Israel, and the country cannot bear what he is saying. This is what he says, that Jeroboam is to die by the sword, and Israel to go into exile, far from its own country. (Amos 7: 10, 11)

TEACHER: Probably not waiting for orders, yet not daring to arrest Amos, the priest rushed into the street and cried:

AMAZIAH: You dreamer! Be off to Judah and earn your living there; play the prophet there, but never again at Bethel, for it is the royal shrine, the national temple. (Amos 7:12, 13)

TEACHER: So Amos returned to his flocks and someone wrote his message as we have it in this book.

WORSHIP IN SHECHEM

There are some stories in our Bible of ancient altars of the Canaanites at which the Hebrews worshiped the Canaanitish gods (Judges 8:33). One of these "high places" was located in Shechem and the god at this place was called Baal-berith or El-berith (Judges 9:4 and Judges 9:46).

After the Hebrews had lived in Canaan for a few hundred years, some of them changed at Shechem to the worship of Yahweh, their volcano and storm god, instead of Baal-berith, the Canaanite god of that ancient altar. We have already seen how the Hebrews grew to believe that Yahweh was one of the baalim of Canaan.

As the years passed by, people tried to explain why there was an altar in Shechem. They said that Yahweh had appeared to Abraham beside a sacred tree at this place. Gradually they had forgotten about the ba'al of the Canaanites and remembered only Yahweh. You will find in your Old Testament the old story which they told to explain why Shechem was a holy place (Genesis 12:6, 7).

In another place, a story is told of Jacob buying a piece of land at Shechem and it says "he erected there an altar and called it ēl the god of Israel" (Genesis 33:20).

WORSHIP AT BETHEL

At Bethel the Canaanites worshiped a spirit, probably because at that spot there were many stones worn into curious shapes by the weather. Since there were no scientists in those faraway times to explain this to the people, they said that it must be caused by a spirit living there. Here also the Hebrews worshiped the ba'al or spirit much as the Canaanites did. But as time passed they changed to the worship of their ba'al, Yahweh, at Bethel just as they had changed at Shechem. When they had forgotten about the worship of the Canaanite spirit and Bethel had become a sacred place for Yahweh, stories began to be told about a god who visited Jacob in a dream. This seemed to explain to the Hebrews the reason for Bethel being a sacred place.

Perhaps you would like to read the story of Jacob's dream in Genesis 28:10-22. In it we find a Hebrew named Jacob dreaming about some angels coming down a ladder from heaven. His strange experience led him to suppose that this place of Luz (meaning the sacred almond tree) was a holy place. So he set up a stone which he had slept upon and said, "this stone, which I have set up for a pillar shall be the house of an ēl or Bethel" (Genesis 28:22).

Later on Yahweh took the place of the ēlim of desert days and became the ba'al of Palestine. There came a day when the Hebrews came to think that he could only be found and worshiped in the land of Canaan or Palestine. (Yet once he had lived only in a volcano in Sinai.) When Naaman of Damascus wanted to worship Yahweh in his own city, he requested that Elisha give him two mules' loads of earth from Canaan to carry home with him to Damascus.

And Naaman said . . . let there be given to thy servant two mules' burden of earth; for thy servant will henceforth offer neither burnt-offering nor sacrifice unto other gods, but unto Yahweh. (II Kings 5:15, 16, 17)

Another old story also shows Yahweh as the god of Canaan. A certain king of Assyria sent some foreign people to live in Palestine. (Read II Kings 17:24-29.) Probably they had tried to worship their own gods. One day they were attacked by some fierce lions and several people were killed. This experience terrified these foreign people. Immediately they thought that they must have offended the god of the land, the god of the Hebrews. Perhaps he was angry with them because they were not worshiping him. When they reported their misfortunes to the king of Assyria, he sent for a Hebrew priest to come and teach them about Yahweh so that he might protect these foreigners from lions and other enemies in Canaan.

PROPHETS URGE PEOPLE TO GIVE UP THEIR HIGH PLACES

We have seen that the Hebrews were learning to worship Yahweh instead of the Canaanite baalim at the high places. Some of the later prophets, such as Micah, saw how often the people were confused in their worship of Yahweh at these places. Often they returned to the worship of the old gods of Canaan, even the sun, moon, and stars (II Kings 18:4, 22). People who have worshiped in one way for hundreds of years do not change easily or quickly. So it was with the Hebrews. The Hebrew prophets spoke again and again to the people about loyalty to Yahweh. In order to overcome these old habits of worship the prophets began to order the destruction of "high places." Then a new law (the Deuteronomic Code) was made to bring the Hebrews to Jerusalem for the worship of Yahweh (about 621 B.C.). Here are some parts of it:

Ye shall surely destroy all the places wherein the nations that ye shall dispossess served their gods, upon the high mountains and upon the hills, and under every green tree; and ye shall break down their altars, and dash in pieces their pillars, and hew down their Asherim; and ye shall burn with fire the graven images of their god; and ye shall destroy their name out of that place. Ye shall not do so to Yahweh your god. (Deuteronomy 12:2-5)

Great ceremonies and special days of festival were to be celebrated in Jerusalem. The religion and worship of Yahweh began to center more and more in this city until finally it became the most holy and sacred city of all Palestine to the Hebrews.[4]

Something to Do

1. Try to find ideas to add to your pictures or your pageant. If you review the religious ideas among the Hebrews in Chart I, you will find considerable help on your plans.
2. Can you think of any ways that people in the present day need to grow or improve in their ideas of God? Perhaps this experience will help you to appreciate the way the ancient Hebrews had to learn what was true and good.
3. Make a list of things which the Hebrews began to think Yahweh could do, after they gave up their worship of the desert ēlim and the baalim of the Canaanites.
4. After the Hebrews began to worship one god, Yahweh, as their god of the land of Canaan, what was the next step necessary to have an idea of God similar to that of Jesus? If you repeat the first words of the Lord's Prayer you may get your answer: "Our Father." To whom is God a Father? Does it make any difference in what part of the world a person lives?
5. What ideas about rain do you find among the ancient Hebrews in their old story of Elijah? I Kings 18:21-46. How have people changed today?
6. What does Amos think about Yahweh? How does he differ from the earlier Hebrews? From Hebrews of his own day?
7. Possibly you may be interested in making a little play from the material on Amos to show some of the ways in which the Hebrews changed in their religion.
8. Read again Amos 5:21-24 to discover some of his ideas of wor-

[4] Even today there are Jews who stand each day beside an ancient part of the wall of Jerusalem and mourn over the loss of the city to them as a center of Jewish worship.

ship. How do they differ from the other Hebrews? What did Jesus seem to think was the best way to worship God? Read these references: John 4:24; Mark 12:38-44; Matthew 5:23, 24.

9. Why did some of the later prophets insist on the Hebrews giving up all of their "high places" of worship except Jerusalem?

CHAPTER XIII: SOME HEBREWS ARE CARRIED AWAY TO BABYLONIA

It was probably between 1400 and 1200 B.C. that the Hebrews began their long struggle to take the land of Palestine away from the Canaanites. About the year 1040 B.C. they were strong enough to elect Saul to be their first king. Under David, their next ruler, the kingdom grew larger and stronger so that most of Canaan was possessed by the Hebrews. When Solomon ruled over this land which his father David had helped to conquer he spent great sums of money for expensive buildings to make Jerusalem a magnificent capital.

People grew discontented when they had to pay heavy taxes to provide this luxury for the king. After the death of Solomon, some of the tribes north of Jerusalem revolted and set up their own kingdom and elected one of their own leaders, Jeroboam, as king. This was known as the kingdom of Israel. Later on the country north of Jerusalem was called Samaria.

Solomon's son Rehoboam became king over the tribes of the south and their kingdom was given the name Judah. This was about 940 B.C., many years after the Hebrews had entered Canaan. Now there were two kingdoms and two capitals, Samaria in the north and Jerusalem in the south.

Dividing this little country of Palestine into two kingdoms made each of them too weak to resist the more powerful countries around them. Frequently they were obliged to pay tribute to Assyria, Egypt or to Babylonia.

Finally a great catastrophe came to the southern kingdom of Judah. One day the Hebrews were horrified to find that Nebuchadnezzar, king of Babylon, and his armies had come up to the walls of Jerusalem. The people were so terrified that they were unable to defend themselves.

And he carried out thence all the treasures of the house of Yahweh, and the treasures of the king's house, and cut in pieces all the vessels of gold which Solomon king of Israel had made. (II Kings 24:13)

He carried away the king and the princes, the craftsmen who would be good workers, and the wealthy people of Jeru-

The Assyrian King, Ashur-nasir-apal developed the art of besieging cities with battering rams and with archers. The battering ram could be wheeled close to a wall and used to batter its foundation. [885-860 B.C.]

salem. They were tied together into a captive train and marched off. Only the poorest Hebrews were allowed to remain. So the leaders of Judah went to live in the land of Babylonia.

It seemed as if Yahweh had forsaken them. One of the prophets, Jeremiah, writes as if Yahweh were saying:

> I have forsaken mine house,
> I have cast off mine inheritance;
> I have given the dearly beloved of my soul
> Into the hands of her enemies. (Jeremiah 12:7)

Their feelings of homesickness and their love for Jerusalem are expressed by these Hebrew captives in Psalm 137.

By the rivers of Babylon,
There we sat down, yea, we wept,
When we remembered Zion.[1]
Upon the poplars in its midst
We hanged up our harps.
For there our captors required of us songs,
And mirth our tormentors:
"Sing us one of the songs of Zion."
How shall we sing Yahweh's songs
In a foreign land? (Psalm 137:1-4)

A SONG OF THE EXILES

One day a group of these sorrowing Jewish pilgrims in the land of Babylon sat down to rest in the shade of a huge willow tree at the side of a stream.

"Here we are, far from our beloved home," said one, "with nobody to tell us of the fate of our friends who were left behind."

"Would that our fathers had heeded the words of the prophets and had ceased their wickedness!" sighed another. "Then should we never have been driven from Zion, the holy hill of Jerusalem. We should be still praising the Lord in his temple instead of mourning here in a strange land."

"Alas, yes," joined in a musician, as he touched the strings of his harp, "how pleasant were the courts of the house of our God! My soul longeth for them again! See, the swallow has found a nest for herself in these branches above, but she is not one half as safe here as were the birds who builded their homes in the altars of our temple. There even the smallest sparrow was safe from all harm. Happy is the man who may still be dwelling there and praising the Lord!"

"Sing us a song about it!" cried the others. "It will make us forget our lonesomeness and feel that we are back again in our beautiful temple, praising God."

So carefully tuning his string, the harper began to play

[1] Zion refers to Jerusalem.

softly in a minor key. Then, gazing thoughtfully up into the silvery green of the willow branches overhead, he sang:

How amiable are thy tabernacles,
O Lord of hosts!
My soul longeth, yea, even fainteth for the courts of the Lord;
My heart and my flesh cry out unto the living God.
Yea, the sparrow hath found her a house,
And the swallow a nest for herself, where she may lay her young,
Even thine altars, O Lord of hosts,
My King, and my God.
Blessed are they that dwell in thy house:
They will be still praising thee.

Nebuchadnezzar claimed the honor of building the city of Babylon so beautifully. Probably he carried the captive Jewish leaders from Jerusalem through this Ishtar gate decorated with sacred bulls and dragons.

At these words he changed to the familiar praise song, and they all joined in eagerly, although some found themselves too sorrowful to sing as in the olden days. Then once more the harper struck into the minor tune and sang a second time alone:

Blessed is the man whose strength is in thee;
In whose heart are the highways to Zion.
Passing through the valley of weeping they make it a place of springs;
Yea, the early rain covereth it with blessings.
They go from strength to strength;
Everyone of them appeareth before God in Zion.
O Lord God of hosts, hear my prayer;
Give ear, O God of Jacob.

Again he stopped, as they all lifted up their hands in supplication, and joined in the prayer song they had always used in the temple. Then for the third time the harper continued:

Behold, O God our shield, and look upon the face of thine anointed.
For a day in thy courts is better than a thousand.
I had rather be a doorkeeper in the house of my God,
Than to dwell in the tents of wickedness.
For the Lord God is a sun and a shield:
The Lord will give grace and glory;
No good thing will he withhold from them that walk uprightly.
O Lord of hosts,
Blessed is the man that trusteth in thee.

And once more the others took up the well-known refrain of rejoicing, almost forgetting as they sang that they were not in their own temple, but rather were out in the land to which they had been brought as captives.

"May it not be," suggested one, as the music died away, "that our God will hear us even here, far from his land as we are?"

"Can we ever hide from his presence?" asked the musician gravely. "If we take the wings of the morning and fly to the uttermost ends of the earth, even there we shall find him. Is not this his temple here, under the vaulted firmament of heaven, as truly as under the bright dome of our temple at

Jerusalem? Do not the heavens declare the glory of God much better than the beauty we have tried to build into his house even?"

"It is truly so, as thou sayest," replied the oldest and wisest of the little group, "and man himself is his handiwork, as well as the heavens above. Therefore let us be fit temples for his praise, no matter where we may dwell. So shall we be all the more worthy of our God, and worthy too to return some day to our homes and the temple on Mount Zion. Who knows?"

"Yes," murmured the others, "we may return again to our temple, some day. Who knows?"

Chart III: Order of Events (Continued)

940 B.C.   The Hebrew kingdom is divided, each with its own king. Israel becomes the northern one and Judah the southern kingdom.

750 B.C.   Amos and Hosea teach loyalty to Yahweh.

722 B.C.   The Assyrians besiege Samaria, capital of Israel. Hebrew leaders are carried away as captives. Assyrians settle foreign people in Israel. They live with the remaining Jews. Later we know them as Samaritans. Isaiah and Micah speak to the Hebrews in the kingdom of Judah about the will of Yahweh.

621 B.C.   Under King Josiah the temple at Jerusalem is rebuilt and reforms are made in the worship. The Deuteronomic code of laws urges the destruction of all high places of worship except at Jerusalem.

604 B.C.   Babylon controls most of the Orient.

586 B.C.   Nebuchadnezzar besieges Jerusalem and destroys it. The Hebrew leaders are carried away as exiles to Babylon. Here some Hebrews grow to believe in one God. An unknown prophet preaches to the exiles. His teachings are found in Isaiah 40-55.

Something to Do

1. Continue working on your pictures or your pageant telling the story of the Hebrew quest for God. Are there any new ideas in this chapter?

2. Why were some of the Jews carried away as captives to Babylon?

3. How did some of these Jewish exiles begin to feel about Jerusalem and their temple?

4. Study Chart III to find the main events in the story of the Hebrew people. Some of the items are new to the story as written in the preceding chapters.

5. If Yahweh had been considered the god of Canaan, what changes would you expect to take place in the thinking of the Hebrew exiles? Perhaps Psalm 139:7-16 and Isaiah 40:30 will help you.

CHAPTER XIV: THE JEWS ARE TO BECOME MISSIONARIES

TEACHINGS OF A GREAT PROPHET

Living as foreigners in the strange land of Babylonia taught some of the Hebrews many things. As they felt the need of their god, Yahweh, a wonderful thing happened. They grew to realize that there is a God of all people in every part of the earth. The words of one of their poets help us to appreciate how much the Hebrews had learned since their ancestors worshiped long ago near Mount Sinai. (Between 1400 and 1200 B.C.) Notice that the writer of this Psalm feels that God is everywhere.

> Where could I go from thy Spirit,
>   where could I flee from thy face?
> I climb to heaven?—but thou art there;
> I nestle in the nether-world?—
>   and there thou art!
> If I darted swift to the dawn,
>   to the verge of the ocean afar,
> thy hand even there would fall on me,
>   thy right hand would reach me.
> If I say "The dark will screen me,
>   the night will hide me in its curtains,"
> yet darkness is not dark to thee,
>   the night is clear as daylight.[1] (Psalm 139:7-16)

About 546 B.C. a great prophet whom scholars call the "Second Isaiah," began teaching many of the very noblest things about God which we know. Though his name has been forgotten, we are glad to have some of the splendid things which he said.

This Second Isaiah taught that there is but one God; that

[1] Moffatt translation.

He is the only true God of the whole world. How much the Hebrews had grown since their days in the desert! He said that Yahweh had directed the world from the very beginning and will continue to do so to the very end.

An eternal God is Yahweh, the creator of the ends of the earth.
(Isaiah 40:30)

This unknown prophet ridiculed the worship of images. He tried to show the people how foolish it was to worship a piece of wood covered over with silver and gold.

The nameless prophet said that the Jews had been chosen to be the servants of Yahweh. They were to be missionaries to all the world in order to help people to understand Yahweh and to worship Him. He encouraged the exiles living in this strange land to understand that their sufferings would be of use to them in bringing others to know Yahweh. He said, Yahweh was permitting innocent people to suffer in order to help them to lead the heathen to know the true Lord. So the Jews were encouraged to be patient in their sufferings in order to show the world the way to the worship of the only true God. He said God called them to be His servants, saying to them:

Thou art my servant; Israel, in whom I will be glorified.
(Isaiah 49:3)

Behold, my servant, whom I uphold,
    My chosen, in whom my soul delights;
I have put my spirit upon him
    he will bring forth justice to the Gentiles.
.   .   .   .   .   .
He will bring forth justice in truth.
    He will not fail nor be discouraged,
Till he has set justice in the earth;
    And the isles shall wait for his instruction.
(Isaiah 42:1-4)

Some day, says this prophet, the people of the world will discover that this suffering of the Jews was for their sakes in order to lead them to God. Then these people will say of the Jews:

Who could have believed that which we have heard?

.   .   .   .   .   .

He (the Jews) had no form nor comeliness, that we
    should look at him,
No beauty, that we should desire him
He was despised and forsaken of men,

.   .   .   .   .   .

Surely, he has borne our sicknesses

.   .   .   .   .   .

But he was wounded for our transgressions,
    he was bruised for our iniquities;

.   .   .   .   .   .

All we like sheep have gone astray,
    we have turned everyone to his own way;
And Yahweh laid upon him the punishment of us all.

(Isaiah 53:1-6)

Sometimes when innocent people have suffered they have
been able to learn some of the very noblest things about God
and His world. Love, forgiveness, courage, and sacrifice are
ways in which God is seen in the lives of people. The nameless
prophet said to the Jews:

Surely, God is in thee, and there is none else,

.   .   .   .   .   .

Verily, with thee God hides Himself,
    the God of Israel, the Saviour[2]

(Isaiah 45:14f)

Now it is well to remember that not all the Jews had such
fine ideas of their religion. Many times they forgot to become
missionaries to other people. Sometimes they became proud
of their own race and of their religion and were prejudiced
against other races and peoples. They rejoiced to think of
God punishing their enemies. They felt delight in revenge
coming to those who had wronged them. But after the exile
there were always some Jews with a nobler understanding of
God. Finally one of the greatest Jewish teachers came. This

[2] See also I John 4:12, 13, 16.

was Jesus and from him the Christians have received the most help in understanding God.

THE SERMON OF JONAH

Two or three hundred years before Jesus was born, a Jew wrote a story which gives the most glorious idea of God found in all the Old Testament.[3] We do not know the name of this great religious teacher but we have his message in our Bible. The title of it is the name of a man called Jonah.

Yahweh had commanded Jonah to go to Nineveh to warn the people against their evil ways. Jonah refused to go and fled in a ship to try to escape the anger of Yahweh. A terrific storm at sea frightened the sailors and they rudely awakened Jonah to pray to his God to save them all. Soon the sailors discovered that the storm had been sent because Jonah was running away from the work of Yahweh.

The storm grew so terrible that the sailors finally threw Jonah into the sea. Then the sea became calm. At the same time a great fish appeared and swallowed Jonah. After three days it cast Jonah out on land. Jonah then went to Nineveh and began warning the people against their wickedness. But when he discovered that Yahweh was not going to destroy the people of Nineveh, he became very angry. He built himself a booth outside the city and waited for Nineveh's destruction. A vine which covered his booth began to wither and die from the scorching east wind. Jonah became even angrier. But Yahweh said to him:

"Thou hast had regard for the gourd, for which thou hast not labored, neither madest it grow . . . and should not I have pity on Nineveh, that great city, in which are more than 120,000 persons that cannot discern between their right hand and their left, and also much cattle?" (Jonah 4:10)

[3] The story of Jonah was probably written about 250 B.C. It was written to satirize Israel for her unwillingness to fulfill her God-given mission to make Yahweh known to the rest of the world. Her suffering was to this end (Isaiah 52:13ff).

Perhaps there was once a person named Jonah who lived four or five hundred years before this story was written. But the great teacher or writer of this book was not concerned about teaching the Jews the history of Jonah, who had lived so long ago. He merely borrowed the name Jonah, which means dove, to use in his great sermon to show them that they should teach even their enemies to know and to worship God. In a few words this is what the writer was trying to tell the Jews:

Yahweh sent the "Dove" (or the Jews) with a message to another country, but she was not willing to go, and so she tried to run away from her task. Then she was punished by being swallowed up in the Babylonian exile, just as Jonah was swallowed up by the whale. In order to teach her a lesson, God marvelously saved her life, and helped her to escape so that she still might carry out her work to bring all the world to know about her God. Finally the "Dove" (or the Jews) did try to help the foreign people a little. But just as soon as she saw them become sorry for their evil deeds and turn to God, she was angry because He did not punish and destroy them. The writer then tried to make the Jews feel ashamed of this selfishness in their worship of God.

The Second Isaiah had dreamed of the time when the Jews would tell all the world about their God. He said:

How beautiful upon the mountains are the feet of him that bringeth good tidings, that publisheth peace, that bringeth good tidings of good, that publisheth salvation, that saith unto Zion, Thy God reigneth! (Isaiah 52:7)

So a few great Jewish teachers realized that there is a God of all people, somewhat as King Ikhnaton of Egypt long ago had believed Aton to be. But these Jewish teachers considered it the high privelege of their people to become missionaries to help the other people of the world to know their God and to grow like Him in their living.

For the love of God is broader than the measure of man's mind,
And the heart of the Eternal is most wonderfully kind;
But we make His love too narrow by false limits of our own,
And we magnify His strictness by a zeal He will not own.

—F. W. Faber

Something to Do

1. What are the noblest ideas of God that you have ever discovered? Make a chart and place all the primitive ideas of God on one side and the nobler ideas on the other side of the line.
2. When people worship a God of all people, how do you think people should treat each other?
3. What did the great prophet, Second Isaiah, teach the Jews to think about their sufferings and their exile?
4. What missionary work did the unknown writer of Jonah and of Second Isaiah believe the Jews should do? What did many Jews think about these teachings?
5. Talk with some Jews today and try to discover what they believe their religious work is now.

CHAPTER XV: TEACHING FRIENDSHIP FOR FOREIGNERS

In the Bible there are several very interesting stories which have been written to teach the Hebrews something of God. One of these is the story of Ruth.

We have already noticed that the Hebrews learned many things while they were in exile. After some of them had returned to their beloved Palestine, they became devoted to all the Hebrew laws and wished to be very loyal Jews.

Some of these laws had to do with marriage. Ezra, Nehemiah, and other leaders said that the Jews should not marry people of other nationalities.[1]

A few Jews did not agree with this idea. They said that it had been done in the past. To prove this, one writer told the beautiful story of Ruth, who was a foreigner and yet had married a Hebrew and had become the ancestress of the famous king, David. Since all Jews admired David, this lovely story must have been a very impressive way of teaching the Jews that foreigners in the past had married Hebrews and had become the parents of some of their greatest leaders.

RUTH

SCENE I

PLACE: *In Moab, on the road to Judah.*

CHARACTERS: NAOMI, RUTH, ORPAH.

SETTING: NAOMI, RUTH, ORPAH, *are on the road going toward Judah.* (NAOMI *stops and faces about.*)

NAOMI: Turn back, my daughters-in-law; return each of you to your mother's house. You have come with me far enough. I must take the rest of my journey alone.

[1] Ezra 10 and Nehemiah 13:23f.

ORPAH AND RUTH: Oh, do not send us back! We will not leave thee!

NAOMI: Yea, you must leave me now. I am going home to my own country and my own people, to Bethlehem, Judah! It is ten long years since I left there to come to dwell in your land of Moab. But now that famine is over I must return.

ORPAH: But, Naomi, our mother-in-law, we love thee. Do not thou leave us!

NAOMI: I must go. I came to this country happy with my husband and two sons, but misfortune has dealt bitterly with me. My husband first died, and now my two sons, your husbands, are taken from me. I am old and sad. I have no one left to comfort me. I must go back to mine own people. Leave me, my daughters, and God bless you! (*Both daughters weep.*)

ORPAH (*weeping and kissing* NAOMI): If thou wilt be happier, then thou must leave us. I will return to my mother's house as thou sayest. (*She departs slowly.*)

(RUTH *still stands by weeping. Takes hold of* NAOMI'S *hand.*)

NAOMI: Behold, Orpah, thy sister-in-law, has gone back to her people and unto her gods. Return thou after thy sister-in-law.

RUTH: Entreat me not to leave thee, nor to return from following after thee: for whither thou goest, I will go; and where thou lodgest, I will lodge; thy people shall be my people, *and thy God my God*: where thou diest, will I die, and there will I be buried: the Lord do so to me, and more also, if aught but death part thee and me.

NAOMI: Since thou art so steadfastly minded to go with me, Ruth, I will cease urging thee. Come, thou mayest go with me to Bethlehem.

SCENE II

PLACE: *In the barley fields of* BOAZ.
TIME: *The harvest season.*

CHARACTERS: BOAZ, RUTH, HEAD REAPER, REAPERS, GLEAN-ERS. (*The* REAPERS *come in with their sickles, followed by the* GLEANERS.)

HEAD REAPER: Truly we have a wonderful harvest this year.

FIRST REAPER: Yea, we will have food enough for ourselves and for all the poor in our city of Bethlehem.

HEAD REAPER: It is the great God that hath given us this bounty.

(*All sing harvest songs as they reap.* RUTH *comes in and begins to pick up the grain.*)

SECOND REAPER (*looking toward the entrance to the field*): The master is coming, the great Boaz!

(*All* REAPERS *look in that direction as they stand, resting their sickles on the ground.* BOAZ *enters.*)

BOAZ: The Lord be with you!

REAPERS: The Lord bless thee!

(*All go to work again, singing as before.* BOAZ *walks among them; he sees* RUTH *and watches her.*)

BOAZ (*to the* HEAD REAPER): My good man, I would speak a word with thee; come hither.

HEAD REAPER: Speak, O master!

BOAZ: Whose damsel is this that gathereth grain after the reapers?

HEAD REAPER: My master, she is Ruth from Moab, that came back with Naomi, thy kinswoman. She hath been gleaning here since early morning.

BOAZ: Go, bid the reapers not to harm her, and bid them let fall purposely some of the handfuls of grain for her.

(*The* HEAD REAPER *bows low and returns to the reapers.*)

BOAZ (*to* RUTH): Hearest thou not, my daughter? Go not to glean in another field, but stay here by my reapers. Let thine eyes be on the reapers, and do thou glean that which they leave behind. When thou are athirst, go unto the vessels and drink that which the young men have drawn.

RUTH (*bows to the ground*): Why have I found such favor in thine eyes, seeing that I am a stranger in the land?

BOAZ: It has been told me of thy great kindness to thy mother-in-law, Naomi; how thou didst leave thine own people to come with her and be among strangers; and how thou didst leave thy gods to take the God of the children of Israel. This God will bless thee for this.

RUTH: I thank thee, O great Boaz, for thou hast comforted me and thou hast spoken friendly words unto me.

BOAZ: Come hither at meal times and eat of the bread and dip thy morsel in the vinegar with my reapers.

(*The reapers have departed.* BOAZ *goes off.*)

RUTH: Thy God is truly good unto me!

SCENE III

PLACE: *At the gate of the city.*

CHARACTERS: BOAZ, a COUSIN *of* NAOMI, TEN CITIZENS, RUTH, NAOMI. (*Several citizens stand in groups, talking.* BOAZ *enters.*)

BOAZ (*speaks to one of the group*): Hast thou seen my cousin pass this way? I am seeking him.

FIRST CITIZEN: Nay, good sir, I have not seen him.

BOAZ: I must speak with him; I will wait here by the city gate; perchance he will come soon.

(*One or two citizens pass by and speak to* BOAZ. *Enter* KINSMAN.)

BOAZ: Ho, Kinsman, turn aside! I would have a word with thee. Sit thee down.

(KINSMAN *sits down.*)

KINSMAN: What wilt thou, Cousin?

BOAZ: I would speak about a matter of importance; wait thou here until I can bring witness. (*He turns to citizens.*) A piece of land is about to be sold; will ten citizens witness this deed?

CITIZENS: Ay, indeed. (*They come forward.*)

BOAZ: Sit ye down here. (*They sit down.*) (*To* KINSMAN.) Dost thou remember Naomi, our kinswoman, who went with her husband and two sons to the land of Moab?

KINSMAN: Yea, I do know Naomi.

BOAZ: She selleth a parcel of land which was her husband's. Now, thou art nearest kin to Naomi, so I thought to advise thee that thou mayest have the first chance to redeem the land in the presence of the elders of the city. If thou dost not care to redeem it, then the right to redeem it cometh to me, for I am next kin. What wilt thou do?

KINSMAN: I will buy the land from our kinswoman, Naomi.

BOAZ: On the day that thou buyest the field from the hand of Naomi, thou also takest Ruth, the Moabitess, for thy wife, according to our custom and law.

KINSMAN: Then I will not redeem the land, for I cannot take Ruth, for my wife. Take thou my right to redeem it and buy it for thyself.

BOAZ (*taking off his shoe and giving it to the* KINSMAN, *he says to the witnesses*): Ye are witness this day that I have bought this parcel of land from Naomi and that I buy also, as my wife, Ruth, the daughter-in-law of Naomi. Of all this ye are witnesses.

CITIZENS: We are witnesses. (*Bow.*)

(KINSMAN *returns shoe to* BOAZ *and walks off.* RUTH *and* NAOMI *come through the street.*)

BOAZ: Ye are well met, Naomi, my kinswoman, and Ruth. I have good news for you: I have bought your land and I can now take Ruth for my wife. Come, all ye fellow citizens, for the wedding feast is prepared at my house! (*Takes* RUTH *by the hand.*)

NAOMI: Blessed am I that I should live to see this good thing come to pass! Our God hath been most gracious unto me!

END

So Boaz and Ruth were married. Later, they had a son born to them and this brought great joy, especially to Naomi. They called him Obed. Years afterward, when Obed was grown up and married, he had a son whose name was Jesse. Now Jesse was the father of David, who became the second king of the Hebrews. In this way the writer of the story of Ruth tried to teach the Jews that God did not disapprove of foreigners as such. How could He if He is the God of all people!

But this nobler view of foreigners in the book of Ruth did not appeal to the leaders of the Jews. There was naturally bitter conflict about foreigners and many Jews became more prejudiced than before.

Down through the centuries there have always been people who have been prejudiced against foreigners. We are sorry that there are many people like that today. Jesus seemed to love all kinds of people. Some of his disciples learned to be friendly to foreigners. In our New Testament we read that Peter said, "I see quite plainly that God has no favorites, but that he who reverences Him and lives a good life in any nation is welcomed by Him" (Acts 10:34, 35).

An ancient writer of India wrote this poem to prejudiced people:

See Thyself

In thee,
In me,
In all men,
There dwelleth the One God;

In all
He suffers
And he suffers
For all;

In all everywhere,
See thyself;
Abandon this thy ignorant conceit,
Which holds that thou art separate from other men.[2]

---

[2] An ancient Sanskrit poem, translated by M. K. Ghandi.

Something to Do

1. What work have you yet to do on your pictures or your pageant of the Hebrew quest for God?

2. As the Hebrews developed into a nation, believing in one God, what did they think of foreigners? Read Nehemiah 13:23, 24. If God is a God of all people, what difference would it make whether the Hebrews married foreign wives? What did the writer of Ruth think? How does this writer differ from the viewpoint of D (Deuteronomy 21:10-13)? Compare the attitude toward foreigners revealed by the author of Ruth and the ideas of the Hebrews in the time of Moses.

3. How did Jesus feel about foreigners? Read Luke 10:30-36. Why did the Jews consider the Samaritans foreigners? (See Chart III.)

4. What did Peter, one of Jesus' disciples, learn to think about foreigners? See Acts 10:34, 35 and Mark 12:29-31.

5. What do Christians today need to learn about foreigners to be true worshipers of one God?

CHAPTER XVI: OFFERINGS TO THE GODS

Just as people have changed their ideas of God, so have they changed their ideas about sacrifices and offerings. Even today in our churches, people have different reasons for bringing their offerings. Some bring sacrifices and gifts to express thanksgiving; some may offer gifts in order to receive praise and honor from people; some may bring gifts because they believe in this way to win and to keep the favor of God.[1] Others make offerings in order to carry on work in which they believe and in order to carry out God's purposes in the world.

OFFERINGS IN EGYPT

In ancient Egypt there were different kinds of offerings. As centuries passed by, the reasons for bringing them seemed to change. There was a time, if a king died, that incense was burned in order to carry his spirit up to the gods. A few lines from an old Egyptian hymn tells about this:

> The fire is laid, the fire shines;
> The incense is laid on the fire, the incense shines.
> Thy fragrance comes to King Unis, O Incense,
> Thy fragrance of King Unis comes to thee, O Incense.
> Your fragrance comes to King Unis, O ye gods;
> The fragrance of King Unis comes to you, O ye gods.[2]

Many kinds of ceremonies were carried on in Egypt. Some of the offerings were brought to the temple for the gods because it was said, "God knows of the one who does any service for him."

Often it seems as if the gifts were brought in order to win the favor of the gods. Gradually some of the religious leaders began to feel that goodness in the lives of worshipers was the

---

[1] Read what Jesus said about offerings: Matthew 6:2-4.
[2] Breasted, James H., *The Dawn of Conscience*, p. 87.

noblest offering that could be brought to the gods. An ancient Egyptian king said, "More acceptable is the virtue of the upright man than the ox (brought as an offering) of him that doeth iniquity." This king believed in bringing gifts to the god but he considered good lives the most important way to serve his god.

OFFERINGS OF THE GREEKS

The Greeks also were taught that every man should bring an offering to the gods. At proper seasons these offerings were made. The Greeks believed that when anyone had sinned, they could prevent punishment by bringing prayers and gifts and by burning sacrifices. The pleasant odor from the sacrifices went up to the god and was enjoyed by him.

Here is a prayer offered by a Greek person who was about to sacrifice a pig. The pig is given to win the favor of the god of a grove where trees were to be cut down in order to grow foods.

Whether thou art a god or a goddess to whom this grove is sacred, as is proper, to thee is made the . . . sacrifice of a pig for the cutting of this sacred grove and for these ceremonies . . . in offering this pig as a . . . sacrifice I make to thee most pious petitions that thou mayest be kindly . . . toward me, my house, my servants, and my children. Therefore mayest thou be honored by . . . the sacrifice of this pig.[3]

THE BEGINNINGS OF HEBREW OFFERINGS

In the earliest times, very many hundreds of years ago, we have seen that the Hebrews worshiped quite differently from Jews and Christians today. While they were desert people they believed that man and his gods were relatives. It was important to keep this relationship or this bond of kinship as strong as possible. When the early Hebrews killed an animal they ate its flesh in order to make the god come into their own bodies and become a part of them. The blood was poured on the altar

[3] Case, S. J., *Experience with the Supernatural*, p. 166.

where the Hebrews worshiped. In this way the worshiper formed friendship with the god of the place.

Very long ago, in desert life, the owner of a sheep, an ox, or a camel had no right to kill an animal to suit his own pleasure. It was slain so that its life might be distributed between all the relatives and the god of the tribe. No part of the life must be lost. The body of the animal was believed to have life that must be eaten up at once in order to enter into the worshiper's body.

Animals were killed and the blood and fat were given as offerings to Yahweh. Other people, including the Romans, sacrificed animals in their worship.

After a time this custom changed. The blood and fat of the animals were sprinkled or daubed on the worshipers. The people ate the part of the animal where sacred life was believed less present. Finally it became the custom to pour the blood out at the altar and to burn the fat, because the blood was very sacred.

The anointed priest of the Aaronic succession shall offer it by a lasting rule, burning it all to the Eternal.[4] (Leviticus 6:22)

Any male among the priests may eat it: it is most sacred.[5]
(Leviticus 6:29)

Nothing could be left over. The Hebrew law said that what was not eaten on the first or second day must be burned.

[4] The Moffatt translation.
[5] The Moffatt translation.

The flesh of the victim of the recompense-offering which is offered as a thank-offering must be eaten on the day it is sacrificed; nothing must be left over till next morning. (Leviticus 7:15)[6]

When a sheep or an ox was brought to the altar, it became the property of the god. The flesh and the fat was burned on an altar because the Hebrews believed that the god enjoyed these as his food. Offerings were made to keep the god in good humor. When the god became friends with the community, then he entered into all its activities and became the enemy of its enemies.

Part of offering for the priests

In the beginning, all animals sacrificed were eaten by the worshipers. We have noticed that after a time only a part of the animal was eaten and the other part burned and the blood poured out at the altar. After the exile it became the custom to give the flesh to the priests. The offering was considered very holy. For this reason only the priests ate it.

Why have you not eaten the sin-offering at the sanctuary? It is most sacred, and you were given it as food in order that you might remove the guilt of the community, by making expiation for them before the Eternal. (Leviticus 10:17)[7]

Grain and fruit offerings

After the Hebrews came to live in the land of Canaan, they gave up their wandering desert life and settled down to raise grain and fruits. The Canaanites brought the first of the crop as an offering to their gods, so the Hebrews began to do it also.

Offerings to make up for sin

When a person committed an act that was considered a sin, such as murder, the Hebrews believed that the god where they lived became angry with the whole community. The com-

[6] The Moffatt translation.
[7] The Moffatt translation.

munity was obliged to discover the offender and to get rid of him. If he was not found, then a sacrifice was made in order to bring peace between the community and its god.[8]

HUMAN SACRIFICES

Early Semitic peoples had the terrible custom of sacrificing children as offerings to their gods. The Old Testament mentions this in several places: II Kings 17:31, II Kings 3:27, Leviticus 18:21, Leviticus 20:2.

The Hebrews also worshiped by giving their first-born children as a sacrifice to the god. They followed this custom for many hundreds of years. Probably it was not until after the exile that it entirely ceased. See Jeremiah 7:31, Jeremiah 19:5, Ezekiel 20:25, II Kings 3:27. If a sacrifice was required, it was the first-born child who was chosen. Probably this first child was thought the most sacred one (Genesis 40:3). In some of the very oldest laws of the Hebrews it says that the god Yahweh wanted their first-born sons as a sacrifice. Read Exodus 23:9. On very special occasions, adults were offered as a sacrifice to Yahweh (Judges 11:31, 39).

THE CUSTOM OF HUMAN SACRIFICE CHANGES

This dreadful form of worship was carried on by the Hebrews for many hundreds of years. It probably lasted until their leaders were carried away from Palestine to live as exiles in Babylonia. You may read in your Bible what some of the Hebrew kings and leaders did.[9] Here you can feel how much the writer of this old history disapproves of the custom of child sacrifice. When the kings did it, they probably felt that it was a necessary kind of worship. Very gradually people learned that God did not wish them to kill innocent people as offerings. Rams and sheep and oxen were considered a sufficient offering. A great prophet and teacher named Jeremiah said

[8] Deuteronomy 21 tells about this.
[9] II Kings 16:3; 21:6; 23:10.

that the Hebrews had built "high places . . . to burn their sons and their daughters in the fire; which I (Yahweh) commanded not, neither came it into my mind" (Jeremiah 7:31).

The Bible story of Abraham preparing to kill his son Isaac as an offering to his god is told to the later Hebrews to prove that Yahweh no longer required human sacrifices to be made (Genesis 22:1-17).

THE HEBREWS WORSHIP AFTER THE MANNER OF THE CANAANITES

We have noted that the Hebrews who came to live in Canaan considered it necessary to worship the baalim of the land just as the Canaanites had done for hundreds of years before.

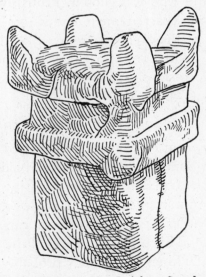

An altar of incense. [See Isaiah 17:8 and 27:9.]

Life in Canaan required that people raise grain, fruits, and other foods. To do this successfully it was necessary to have the favor of the baalim. So it came about that on certain special occasions the farmer brought gifts of grain, or of cakes made from the grain, to the baalim. (See Genesis 4:3, Exodus 23:19, and Judges 6:20.)

YAHWEH PREFERS GOODNESS TO SACRIFICES

We have discovered that it was several hundred years after the time of Moses before there were prophets who thought that Yahweh alone was their god. One said, "What great nation is there, that has a God so nigh unto them, as Yahweh our god is whensoever we call upon him" (Deuteronomy 4:7)? These later prophets felt that the Hebrews should worship Yahweh alone. They said that no other people had ever had such wonderful experiences with Yahweh as the Hebrews. To these prophets it seemed as if Yahweh must *always* have cared for the Hebrews from the very beginning and *always* have been their god.

It was customary for Hebrews to believe that sacrifices were very important in the worship of Yahweh. Yet after the exile a Jewish writer insisted that Yahweh did not wish offerings and sacrifices but justice and goodness. He said, "Seek good and not evil." You can read his words which were later added to the book of Amos (Amos 5:21:25).

Another Jewish writer added to the message of the prophet, Hosea, that Yahweh loved His people. He believed that Yahweh spoke these words to him:

> I desire loving kindness and not sacrifice,
> And the knowledge of God rather than burnt offerings. (Hosea 6:6)

Still another prophet said of Yahweh:

> He has showed thee, O man, what is good, and what does Yahweh require of thee,
> But to do justice, and love kindness, and to walk humbly with thy God.   (Micah 6:6-8)

So Jewish ideas of worship changed very much. Instead of making a gift of an animal or of grain to the gods, some of the great Jews believed that it was more important to bring gifts

of goodness and love. "To do righteousness and justice is more
acceptable to Yahweh than sacrifice" (Proverbs 21:3).

One Jewish Psalm writer also says that animal and grain
sacrifices are of little value to Yahweh.

> Sacrifices and offering
> Thou hast no delight in;
>
> .   .   .   .   .
>
> Burnt-offering and sin-offering
> Thou hast not required.
> (Psalm 40:6)

Another Hebrew writes as if Yahweh, Himself, were speaking and this is what He says:

> I am Yahweh, thy God,
>
> .   .   .   .   .
>
> I will not reprove thee for thy sacrifices;
> Thy burnt-offerings are continually before me
> I will take no bullock out of thy house,
> Nor he-goats out of thy folds,
> For every beast of the forest is mine,
>   and the cattle on the hills of God.
> I know all the birds of the mountains
>   and that which moves in the field is mine.
> If I were hungry, I would not tell thee;
>   for the world is mine, and its fulness,
> Do I eat the flesh of bulls or drink the
>   blood of goats?
> Offer to God the sacrifice of thanksgiving,
>   so wilt thou pay thy vows to the Most High;
> And call upon me in the day of trouble:
> I will deliver thee, and thou shalt glorify me.
> (Psalm 50:7-15)

Still another psalmist says:

> I will praise the name of God with a song,
>   and magnify Him with thanksgiving;
> And it will please Yahweh better than an ox
>   or a bullock that has horns and hoofs.
> (Psalm 69:30)

JESUS' TEACHINGS ABOUT OFFERINGS

Belief in goodness as an offering to Yahweh has been taught by many religious leaders.[9a] Jesus taught that kindness and love were the best gifts to bring to God. Here are some things which it is supposed that Jesus said:

God is Spirit, and his worshipers must worship him in Spirit and in reality.[10] (John 4:24)

So if you remember, even when offering your gift at the altar, that your brother has any grievance against you, leave your gift at the very altar and go away; first be reconciled to your brother, then come back and offer your gift.[11] (Matthew 5:23, 24)

And in the course of his teaching he said, "Beware of the scribes! They like to walk about in long robes, to get saluted in the market places, to secure the front seats in the synagogues and the best places at banquets; they prey upon the property of widows and offer long unreal prayers. All the heavier will their sentence be!"

Sitting down opposite the treasury, he watched the people putting their money into the treasury. A number of the rich were putting in large sums, but a poor widow came up and put in two little coins amounting to a halfpenny. And he called his disciples and said to them, "I tell you truly, this poor widow has put in more than all who have put their money into the treasury; for they have all put in a contribution out of their surplus, but she has given out of her neediness all she possessed, her whole living."[12] (Mark 12: 38-44)

> Not what we give, but what we share,
> For the gift without the giver is bare;
> Who gives himself with his alms feeds three,
> Himself, his hungering neighbor, and me.
> —James Russell Lowell.

Chart IV: Order of Some Events

538 B.C.	Cyrus of Persia takes Babylon. Some Hebrews return to Palestine, and join those who have remained there.

[9a] Psalm 103 stresses this nobler kind of offering.
[10] The Moffatt translation.
[11] The Moffatt translation.
[12] The Moffatt translation.

516 B.C.	The second temple is completed in Jerusalem.
458 B.C.	The Samaritans of the north and the Jews of the south quarrel over the temple.
420 B.C.?	High priests rule the Hebrews more and more. Samaritans build their temple at Mt. Gerizim.
332 B.C.	Alexander the Great (Greek) invades Palestine. Greek influences grow in Palestine.
300-200 B.C.	Jonah story told to teach Hebrews to be missionaries of one God to other people.
175 B.C.	Antiochus Epiphanes compelled Jews to worship Greek gods.
168 B.C.	The Jews rebel against their Syrian oppressors.
166 B.C.	Book of Daniel written to comfort the Jews, during their oppression by the Syrians.
139 B.C.	Rome recognizes the Jewish state in Palestine.
63 B.C.	Pompey of Rome captures Jerusalem.
B.C. (Before Jesus is born)	Jesus is born and teaches.
A.D.	Anno Domini means in the year of our Lord or in the Christian period—after the birth of Jesus.
A.D. 20	Herod rebuilds the temple of Jerusalem. It is the temple known to Jesus.
A.D. 70	Titus from Rome destroys Jerusalem. Jewish temple worship ceases and the Jews are scattered.

Something to Do

1. If you have been making pictures, models, or a pageant illustrating the changes and growth in the Hebrew religion, this chapter will be a review.

2. Make a list of things people have done to win the favor of a god.

3. How does worship change as man's ideas of God grow and change? Review Chart I.

4. Why were human beings sacrificed to a god?

5. What is a nobler way of serving God? Read Amos 5:21-25; Micah 6:6-8; John 4:24.

6. Read Chart IV in order to find out the rest of the events in the Hebrew story.

CHAPTER XVII: PRAYER

Man has said prayers to the gods for many purposes. Sometimes these prayers have been noble but very often they have been selfish and cruel. Even today, people repeat selfish prayers and expect God to give them gifts because they ask for them. But there have been in the past and are in the present, other people who pray to God in order to become more like Him in goodness. A man once said that he "who rises from prayer a better man, his prayer is answered."[1]

A GREEK PRAYER

Notice this noble prayer offered long ago by a Greek whose name is not known:

May I never devise evil against any man, if any devise evil against me, may I escape uninjured and without the need of hurting him. May I love, seek, and attain only to that which is good. May I rejoice for all men's happiness and envy none. May I never rejoice in the ill fortune of one who has wronged me. . . . May I to the extent of my power, give all needful help to my friends and to all who are in want. When visiting those in grief may I be able by gentle and healing words to soften their pain. May I accustom myself to be gentle and never be angry because of circumstances. May I never discuss who is wicked and what wicked things he has done, but know good men and follow in their footsteps.[2]

In the Old Testament we find a prayer which is so beautiful that it reminds us of Jesus.

> Create in me a clean heart, O God
> And renew a right spirit within me.
> Cast me not away from thy presence,
> And take not thy holy spirit from me.
> (Psalm 51:10, 11)

[1] Clodd, Edward, *The Childhood of the World*, p. 159.
[2] *Ibid.*

PRAYERS OF REVENGE BY THE HEBREWS

There are other prayers in the Bible that have the spirit of revenge and hatred. As you read them, compare them with the words of Jesus, when he said, "Love your enemies, and pray for them that persecute you" (Matthew 5:44).

There were Hebrews who lived many hundreds of years before Jesus' time who prayed to Yahweh to bring harm to their enemies.

> Let burning coals fall upon them:
> Let them be cast into the fire,
> Into deep pits, whence they shall not rise.
> > (Psalm 140:10)

> I hate them with perfect hatred;
> They are become mine enemies.
> > (Psalm 139:22)

> Let his days be few;
> Let another take his office.
> Let his children be fatherless,
> And his wife a widow.
>
> .   .   .   .
>
> Let there be none to extend
>   kindness unto him;
> Neither let there be any to
>   have pity on his fatherless children.
> > (Psalm 109:8, 9, 12)

WAR PRAYERS

People in the present as well as the past have often believed that their gods would help them in their wars and give them victory over their enemies. Before they went to war, the Romans always prayed to their gods for victory over their enemies. Scipio, on setting sail to attack Carthage, prayed all the gods to bring him and his companions back home again safe and unhurt, victorious over the enemy, decorated with spoils and loaded with booty.

The Hebrews also believed that Yahweh would help them

in their wars. One Hebrew said this about Yahweh and his
enemies:

> Yahweh will swallow them up in his wrath,
>
> .   .   .   .
>
> Thou wilt make ready with thy bowstrings
>   against their face.
>   (Psalm 21:9, 12)
> Yahweh is my strength and song,
>
> .   .   .   .
>
> This is my god, and I will praise him;
>
> .   .   .   .
>
> Yahweh is a man of war:
> Pharaoh's chariots and his host hath
>   he cast into the sea;
>
> .   .   .   .
>
> Thy right hand, O Yahweh, dasheth in
>   pieces the enemy.
>   (Exodus 15:2, 3, 4, 6)

We know that the American Indians prayed to their gods for
help in wars. They prayed to Wohkonda to help them take
scalps and to capture horses.

Even today when civilized people go to war, they pray that
God will help them. Very slowly, however, some Christian and
some Jewish people are beginning to believe that there is one
God and that He is the friend of all people. He is not a God of
war but a God of love. The Friends or Quakers have believed
this for a long time.

PRAYERS OF THE GREEKS

The Greeks offered many prayers to their gods. They asked
them for help in everything they did. In a court of justice, a
popular gathering, or a festival, they always opened the meeting with prayer.

Socrates was a noble Greek teacher. He taught that a farmer
who desired a good year, should pray to the gods for a good

harvest, for increase of his flocks, for the prevention of disease for horses, sheep, cattle, and for protection of his crops.

ROMAN PRAYERS

The Romans were also careful to say prayers for their needs. There were definite prayers for all kinds of problems of the farmer. When clearing a new piece of land, or planting the seed, or gathering the harvest, or caring for the herd, all required certain prayers to the gods.

PRAYERS FOR THE WEATHER

In times of drought, people all over the world have asked their gods to send rain. In America in 1934, there were people who gathered in churches and asked God to send rain.[3] Drought and floods and storms have often seemed like punishment sent by the gods. There are people today who believe this.

PRAYERS OF CO-OPERATION WITH A GOD OF LOVE AND ORDER

There are some people, however, who believe that the true God in the universe is a spirit of goodness and love and that He works in orderly ways. Therefore, when men pray they should try to become like this God and learn to be unselfish, friendly, and co-operative in the ways they use His laws. Instead of asking God to give food and clothing or to stop floods or to send rain in times of drought, men should try to work together to prevent these conditions and to deal with the causes of their difficulties. Unselfish love for the good of all and an intelligent understanding of the world in which we live should lead us to seek in our prayers ways of working and thinking with God.

Perhaps prayers of co-operation would mean that people should pray for enough love for each other to work together to stop floods. It might mean that some should pray for enough

[3] See the story of Elijah in Chapter XII.

love and justice to give work and wages to people to buy their own food and clothing. It would mean that people should pray for enough love for others to co-operate in making a nation and a world where everyone has a chance to live comfortably and nobly.

Instead of asking God to feed and clothe people or instead of asking Him to change the laws of nature, perhaps man needs to learn to pray for love and goodness enough to work with other people to change the conditions which cause suffering and misery.

God is a Spirit, a Spirit of love,
A Spirit of truth, of kindness of joy,
Wherever these are,
    We find God.[4]

O may our eyes be open, Lord,
    To see our neighbor's need,
And may our ears be kept alert
    Their cries for help to heed.
Make keen our minds to plan the best
    For another's good,
That all the world shall be at last
    One friendly neighborhood.[5]

He prayeth well, who loveth well
Both man and bird and beast;
He prayeth best, who loveth best
All things both great and small;
For the dear God who loveth us,
He made and loveth all.
                    —Samuel Coleridge

Something to Do

1. Continue working on any pictures, slides, or pageant which you are creating to tell the story of the Hebrew quest for God.
2. Make a list of different kinds of prayers. What idea of God is in each? Which are the noblest ones? Which make God something like a magician?

[4] Perkins, J. E., *As Children Worship*, p. 76.
[5] *Ibid.*, p. 70.

3. Which prayers are best suited to our modern knowledge of science?

4. Which are nearer to the religion of Jesus? See Luke 6:27-29, 35; John 4:24.

5. Write a prayer to use in your worship service. Find out first what the service will be about.

CHAPTER XVIII: PLACES OF WORSHIP

People have had many different kinds of places of worship. These have depended upon their beliefs about the gods. When it was thought that a spirit lived in a stone or a tree, then offerings and prayers were made to the stone or stump. When people believed that a god lived within an image of some kind, then they worshiped the spirit within it.

STONES USED FOR WORSHIP

All over the world, and for many reasons, stones have been worshiped. In Africa there is a place where food and drink are given to sacred stones in order to cure sick people. Long ago, before Jesus was born, the Romans carried a small black stone image of the goddess Cybele to help them to victory in their wars.

Stones built up like tables and in circles are found in many places. They were often used to mark a burial place, and people worshiped at these places either to pay honor to the dead or because of their fear of them.

WORSHIP IN THE DESERT

People have had curious beliefs about the way their gods associate with man. Nature is mysterious. Early man did not have our modern ideas of science. So he tried to explain everything as showing the presence of a god.

Gods were supposed to live in certain places. Here they had power over the people and over the land. When a stranger came to a new part of the Desert of Arabia, it was the custom to seek the protection of the god of that place. If a man was away from home, he considered himself far away from his own god. It was necessary to seek the friendship of the god while traveling in his land. Man tried to win the favor of his gods in order to get them to do what he desired them to do. Certain ceremonies were carried out as a means of gaining the god's protection.

A SANCTUARY OR A "HIGH PLACE"

A place inhabited by a god was "sacred" which means "set apart." It was considered dangerous to touch anything "sacred." Sometimes persons were put to death after they had touched a "sacred" thing because it was feared that they might harm other people.

These "sacred" places or the homes of the gods were called *sanctuaries*. In order to guard or protect the holiness of such a spot, a wall or line of stones was placed around it. In Canaan such a spot was known to the Hebrews as a "bāmā" or a "high place."

In the Bible there are numerous references to the "high place" as a place of worship. (See I Samuel 9:12; I Kings 3:2; II Kings 23:5.) These "high places" contained pillars made of stone, and asherim made of wood.

THE "HIGH PLACE" AT GEZER

One of the oldest places of worship in Palestine is a cave at Gezer. It was thirty-two feet long, twenty feet broad, and nearly eight feet high. Perhaps at one time the cave dwellers believed that a god lived here. When they killed their offering the blood would run through the place beneath. Here the god was supposed to dwell.

Gezer became one of the high places of worship for the Canaanites. It was surrounded by a stone wall and probably had the following parts:

1. An altar on which to sacrifice the offerings to the god.
2. Some standing stones.
3. Some asherim—either wooden poles or trees.

4. A laver for the washing of the worshiper or the priest.

5. A sacred cave.

6. A place for refuse.

Gezer seems to have had ten standing stones. Eight are still there. The tallest stone is almost eleven feet high. These stones or pillars stand in a row extending north and south.

Gezer is a very ancient high place of worship which was probably used by the Canaanites or by some Hebrew tribe long before the Israel tribe came up from Egypt.

The smallest stone may have been the most sacred one. On top of it are certain smooth spots. These remind us of spots on stones in other holy places that have been worn smooth by the kisses of the worshipers. Many people have worshiped by kissing stones and images in which they believed their gods dwelt. Perhaps some of the blood and the fat from the sacrifices was smeared over certain stones.

We know that the Hebrews also worshiped ba'al in sacred

pillars. We remember that Jacob had a dream about some angels coming down a ladder from heaven. He decided that the place where he had slept was the home of a god. So he put up a stone and called it the house of god (Genesis 27:22).[1]

In the "high place" near the pillars there was probably an asherah or wooden pillar to represent a sacred tree. This custom goes back to tree worship.[2]

The altar was an important part of a high place. We can no longer find it at Gezer. Probably these ancient altars were a mere heap of earth, or a pile of stones or baked clay. In Exodus we find this law about the altar of the early Hebrews:

An altar of earth thou shalt make for me, and shalt sacrifice thereon thy burnt offerings, and thy peace offerings, thy sheep, and thine oxen: in every place where I record thy name I will come unto thee and I will bless thee. And if thou make me an altar of stone, thou shalt not build it of hewn stones; for if thou lift up thy tool upon it, thou hast polluted. (Exodus 20:24, 25)

The burnt sacrifices made by people like Gideon were on a bare rock (Genesis 8:20 and 12:9).

In I Kings 18, there is an account of Elijah's altar being simply a circle marked out by twelve standing stones in a trench.

Just back of the pillars at Gezer was found a square stone with a deep hole cut out of the center of it.[3] Probably this stone was a laver, where people could sit to wash their feet and cleanse themselves before worship.

A little to the east of the sacred cave was a deep pit. In it were found the bones of human beings, cows, sheep, goats and deer. These may have been used as offerings and sacrifices in worship thousands of years ago. Many skeletons of infants have

[1] There came a time when certain leaders tried to teach the Hebrews a better way to worship. Read I Kings 19:18 and Hosea 13:2; Exodus 23:24.

[2] We have seen that the Hebrews also had sacred trees. After a time their leaders taught them to worship in other ways. Read Judges 6:25, 28 and II Kings 17:10.

[3] The stone measures 6 feet, 1 inch by 5 feet by 2 feet, 6 inches, and the hollow inside is 2 feet, 10 inches by 1 foot, 11 inches by 1 foot, 4 inches.

been found. First-born children were considered the most sacred gift for the gods.[4]

In the springtime and in the autumn, the people near Gezer came to celebrate their ancient harvest festivals and to make their offerings. Here the stories of the people were repeated and their religious beliefs passed on to their children.

CEREMONIES AT A HOLY PLACE

Before entering the holy place, the worshiper prepared himself by fasting and by special washing, in order to remove anything from his body which might displease the god. He also removed his garments and his sandals. On entering the sacred place, he covered his head with a cloth or with his hands, so as to avoid the risk of looking at the god. To let the god know of his appearance, he also cried out that he was coming. Then he danced or marched around the holy stone or tree shouting the name of the god as he went. After this he stood still before it in a reverent attitude. If no harm came to him, the worshiper ventured to stroke or to kiss the holy stone.

Following all of this approach to the god, the worshiper killed a first-born animal or first-born child. The blood was given to the gods by being poured on the ground or upon the holy stone. Probably in the beginning there were no altars.

The worshiper ate the meat of the animal at the holy place, believing that the god and himself were joined together physically by eating together. When the worshiper was united with the god into one body then he could expect the help of the god in this particular place.

Early people generally brought, as offerings, those things which were most valuable to them, such as food, for it was believed that this was really the food of the gods. After the sacrifice was completed, prayer was said asking for the favor and help of the god and making promises. If he granted their favor,

[4] See Jeremiah 7:31, Exodus 13:13, Leviticus 18:21, II Kings 16:3, and Micah 6:7.

sometimes it was the custom of the worshiper to offer curses upon his enemies.

Some great pyramids of Egypt.

THE PYRAMIDS OF EGYPT

The gigantic pyramids of Egypt were built of massive stones to house the bodies of their kings, and near them were built great temples. Here priests were hired to present offerings and to perform ceremonies which would help the king in the world of the dead. Such temples were more often places to help the dead rather than the living.

TEMPLES IN BABYLON

To the east of Palestine was the powerful country of Babylon. These people also worshiped many gods. At first there was a god for every river, a sky god, a moon god, a storm god, and so on. Later on, it was believed that there were special gods in each place to help people even in their fields and crops and other problems of living.

The Babylonians said that the gods were lonely without temples and men to worship in them. So men were created. In return for their worship, the gods helped man in their crops, their wars, and their business.

THE TEMPLE AT PETRA TO AN UNKNOWN GOD

People have built many kinds of temples to their gods. In Petra, a desert city south of Palestine, one may find today the ruins of some of these temples which were built by different people in the long past. One of these is cut out of a rocky cliff.[5]

GREEK AND ROMAN TEMPLES

The Greek and Roman temples were among the most beautiful buildings in the ancient world. Every god had its own temple. To these places of worship gifts and sacrifices were brought for the gods.

THE HEBREW TEMPLE TO YAHWEH

Already it has been suggested that the reason for Jerusalem becoming a holy city goes back to the time when men first made offerings on a great rock on one of its hills. This rock has been sacred to many people who have lived in Palestine. Today, it is sacred to the Mohammedans. Probably the rock was used by the priests of the Hebrew temple as the altar of sacrifice for their offerings to Yahweh.

One time when a great army was destroying the country south of Jerusalem probably a plague broke out among the soldiers. Something mysterious happened because Jerusalem was saved from the invaders. More than ever the Hebrews felt that Jerusalem was the special city of Yahweh.

When Solomon became the Hebrew king, he copied the ways of other kings around him and built for himself and his queen a very rich and beautiful palace in Jerusalem. Just be-

[5] See the *National Geographic Magazine* for February, 1935, for many pictures of ancient Petra.

hind it, on the very top of the hill, he built a tiny royal chapel or temple.[6] Very likely it was fashioned after the style of some temples built for the baalim of the Philistines, or the gods of

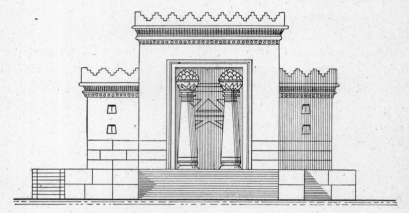

This is a front view of Solomon's Temple.

Egypt. Solomon's temple had a porch at one end and smaller rooms around the main building.

In the court were objects of bronze. Southeast of the temple was an enormous bronze bowl which measured fifteen feet across and seven and a half feet high. It rested on twelve enormous oxen (II Kings 16:17). At the front of the temple were two stone pillars with tops of lily-work. Probably these were relics of the days when people worshiped stone pillars.

Certain important visitors might enter the larger outer room of Solomon's temple. There was a dim light which came through the barred windows. At the far end of this room stood an altar covered with gold. Double folding doors of olive wood, with fine carvings on them, led into a very holy place about thirty feet square. Touching its gilded walls were the outstretched wings of two cherubs covered with gold. These golden-winged creatures were probably much like the winged bulls worshiped in Assyria. An ark of Yahweh was brought

[6] Solomon's temple was ninety feet long, thirty feet wide, and forty-five feet high.

from a tent place of worship in Shiloh and placed under the wings of the cherub.

After seven years of building the first Hebrew temple was ready for use. Solomon built temples to other gods but in later times the Hebrews always praised him because of his temple for Yahweh.

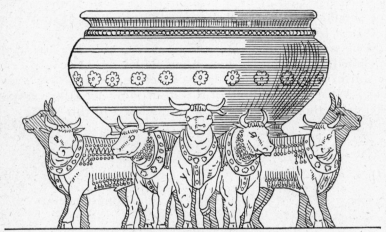

The laver in Solomon's Temple.

When the temple was dedicated King Solomon recited these lines:

Yahweh hath placed the sun in the heavens,
He hath said he would dwell in thick darkness;
I have built thee a house, exalted,
The place of thy dwelling forever.

Something to Do

1. Continue working on the play or the pictures which you have started. What new ideas do you find in this chapter for your plans?
2. Write down all the reasons which you have discovered for people's belief in sacred or holy places. Read again Chapters I to IV and XI.
3. What are some differences between our thinking today about churches and the ideas of the Hebrews long ago about their places of worship? What did they hope to accomplish when they per-

formed ceremonies at these sacred places? Why do we go to our churches?

4. Make a list of differences between the ideas of God found among the early Hebrews and the loftier ideas of some of the prophets after the exile and of Jesus. What differences would such changes in thinking tend to make in worship?

5. Why should people in a modern day worship? Do we need to try to change God or to change ourselves? If the latter, in what ways should we expect to be changed? Read John 4:24, Matthew 5:23, 24, I John 3:18; 4:7-12; 5:20 and Matthew 6:33.

6. Some young people were studying about the church and they concluded: "The church should be a fellowship of people seeking the spirit of God and learning to express it in their everyday relations." What do you think of this idea? How does this viewpoint differ from those of earlier peoples discussed in this book?

CHAPTER XIX: PLACES OF WORSHIP (*Continued*)

After many hundreds of years, when Jerusalem was the holy city of the Hebrews, the temple became the most important place to worship God.

There came a day when Solomon's beautiful little temple to Yahweh was destroyed. We have noticed that Nebuchadnezzar, king of Babylon, beseiged Jerusalem in 586 B.C., captured it, burnt the city, the palaces and the temple, broke down the walls, plundered the gold and silver treasures in the temple and the king's palace, and carried away many of the leaders of the Hebrews as captives to Babylonia.

Assyrian officials conduct a captive king, his daughter, and two sons to King Ashur-nasir-apal. [885-860 B.C.] Probably some of the Jewish exiles were led into Babylon in this manner.

In this strange land many Jews recalled Yahweh with gratitude and were very sad when they remembered that they could no longer go to worship in their temple.

It was more than fifty years before any of the Jews were permitted to return to their homeland. Then one of the first things that they did was to set about rebuilding the temple at Jerusalem. When their new temple was completed (about 516 B.C.)

there was great rejoicing among the Jews. You may read of some of their happiness in Psalm 100:

> O go your way into his gates with thanksgiving,
> And into his courts with praise;
> Be thankful unto him, and speak good of his name.
>
> (Psalm 100:4)

During the exile the Jewish leaders had been gathering together their religious laws. These were probably what we have in the first five books of our Bible.

After hundreds of years in the land of Palestine the Hebrews had come to have many religious laws. These laws explained how to worship in the temple, the duties of all the priests, how to keep the Sabbath, and how to carry out different ceremonial days.

So many laws had been made for Jewish people to follow that worship became very formal. Priests and worshipers had to consult these laws and obey every detail. So the temple became a place for elaborate religious ceremony.

About one hundred and fifty years before Jesus was born, the Jews were under the Greek rule of King Antiochus Epiphanes. He tried to destroy the Jewish temple worship and compel the people to worship like the Greeks. Loyal Jews who refused to change their worship were made to suffer severely. For many years the Jews struggled to worship their own God in their own temple.

There seemed to be no peace for the Jews in the little land of Palestine. In 63 B.C. the Romans became their rulers. In 39 B.C., when Herod was king, he rebuilt the temple at Jerusalem, making it larger and richer than it had been in the days of Solomon. It was to this temple that Jesus came to worship at the age of twelve (Luke 2:41-52).

After the death of King Herod, the Roman rulers grew more cruel and severe. When their treatment seemed unbearable, the Jews rebelled. This ended in a terrible war with the Romans. Seventy years after Jesus' death, Titus, the Roman emperor, destroyed Jerusalem. The beautiful temple built by Herod was burned and torn down. A few of its treasures were taken to Rome.

Never again have the Jews ruled in Palestine. Many Jews in our day are returning to their beloved land of Palestine to live, because all Jews still love this land of their fathers. For nearly two thousand years they have had no temple. They have worshiped in synagogues and have come to believe that God can be found wherever people seek to do His will.

THE FIRST JEWISH SYNAGOGUES

No one really knows exactly where and when the first Jewish synagogue was built. Quite probably it was first built by some of the Jews who had been carried away as captives to live in foreign lands. At different times Jews were carried away from Palestine as captives by their conquerors. Some people think it was in this land of Babylonia while some of the Jewish leaders were held as captives that they first built synagogues because they had no temple. No one knows when the synagogue was first used. But there came a time when the synagogue was the Jewish center of worship and of their religion in a foreign land. It helped the Jews to keep their religion and to continue to worship God as they had in Palestine.

There were synagogues in many towns and cities in the time of Jesus. If you read Matthew 13:54, Mark 6:2, Luke 4:16 and Luke 5:7, you will find references to some of these synagogues in the time of Jesus. Today, the most ancient synagogues have disappeared. It was the custom to build the synagogue in the highest part of the town so that it rose above the other buildings. The oldest synagogues that have been discovered are oblong or rectangular in shape. The ornaments were such Jewish symbols as the seven-branched candle stick. A wreath supported by two figures has been found over the door of one. It had three doorways and in front of them across the synagogue was a portico supported by columns. The doors faced to the west, and the ark was at the eastern end of this synagogue. In most synagogues the doors were placed opposite the Ark and in that part of the room toward which the worshipers faced in prayer.

The synagogue was probably used first by Jews in exile who could not worship at the temple of Jerusalem.

There was a platform in the middle of the house so that the person who read from the scrolls of the Law or who spoke to the people, could be easily heard. This pulpit is called the *alemar*. The sides of the pulpit were open. There were several steps up to it. The desk was covered with rich drapery.

Every synagogue probably had an ark, for the scrolls of the Law and other sacred books which were kept in linen cloths and in a case. The ark was placed in a shutoff part of the synagogue. In front of this hung a curtain. Lamps were used to light the synagogues.

The men sat in the space on either side of the pulpit, while the women were above in a gallery by themselves. The chief seats of the synagogue were in front of the ark facing the people. Men called elders, who were held in the highest honor, sat in these seats. The other people sat in rows, one behind the other, all with their eyes turned toward the elders and toward the Holy Place. In Palestine, long ago, they probably sat on the floor.

Already we have noticed that the first synagogues watched over the training of people in their religious laws. In it other laws were made to help Jews to be more faithful in their religion. Men called elders sat in the synagogue on the second and fifth days of the week to judge people and to decide punishment for offenders.

WORSHIP IN THE SYNAGOGUES

There was no priest or minister or rabbi, such as churches and synagogues have today. A man called a ruler looked after the service of worship on the Sabbath day (Luke 13:14 and Mark 5:22).

The service of the synagogue was in five parts:

1. The men recited the Shema (Deuteronomy 6:4-9 and 11:13-21, Numbers 15:37-41).

2. Prayer was offered by some one chosen by the ruler of the synagogue. The people listened silently and repeated "Amen" at the close. The person who prayed stood in front of the ark.

3. Parts of the Law from the Old Testament were read from a large scroll. On the Sabbath day at least seven persons were called upon by the rulers of the synagogue to read a few verses from the Law. Any member of the congregation could be chosen to read. After each reading there was a benediction (Acts 13:15).

4. Parts of the Prophets from the Old Testament were read. (See Luke 4:16-20.)

5. A sermon followed the reading from the Law and the Prophets. The preacher was seated during his sermon (Luke 4:20-29).

6. A blessing concluded the service.

Though people have worshiped God in trees and stones, on high places, in arks, before images, in temples, synagogues and churches, it is important to remember that God is spirit and that the place or the method of worship is not nearly so important to God as the way people live together. The spirit of goodness and of love counts more in the worship of God than offerings and ceremonies.

When the followers of Jesus began to study his teachings and to preach to Gentiles (people who were not Jews) they had to build new places for their meetings. So they began to build churches. At first these were much like synagogues. Then they changed from the Hebrew style and began to imitate patterns of architecture in the lands where they were built. So today we can find a great many styles of churches in Europe and in America.

Something to Do

1. Review the growth of the Hebrew religion in Chart I. What new materials have you found for your play or your pictures?

2. How many temples did the Hebrews have in Jerusalem? Why was the first one built? What was the purpose of these temples? Review Chapters XI and XVI. Read one story told by Nehemiah of the building of the second temple—Zerubbabel's temple (Nehemiah 2:1-20 and 10:32-39).

3. What criticisms did Jesus make of the temple in his time (Herod's temple)? Mark 12:38-44; Matthew 23:1-7, 23; Matthew 5:23, 24; Mark 11:15-19.

4. Why were synagogues built? What are they used for today? Try to read With Jewish Child in Home and Synagogue, by Elma Levinger.

5. Read a story of Jesus' experience in a synagogue in Luke 4:15-39.

6. Write down what you consider the most important purpose of a house of worship.

CHAPTER XX: THE SABBATH DAY AND SUNDAY

If you know any Jewish people you will remember that their Sabbath day comes on Saturday. It is difficult to find out just how and when this day of worship was first kept.

THE BABYLONIAN SABBATH

Resting on every seventh day seems to have been started very long ago. Probably the Hebrews were not the first people to keep the Sabbath as a holy day. Scholars tell us that the Babylonians kept this day and called it Sabattu. They said it was "a day of rest for the heart." On this day, people were forbidden to eat cooked meat, to put on fresh clothing, to offer sacrifice, to ride in their chariots, or to do any kind of work.

WORSHIP OF THE MOON

Probably the Sabbath was first kept sacred as a time to worship the moon at the four times in each month when it entered its different quarters. Again we must remind ourselves that the people long ago did not have scientists and teachers to give them the facts which everyone can know today about the earth, the sun, the moon, and the stars.

To the Semites, living near the desert or in very warm places, the sun with its hot, burning rays was not so friendly as the moon with its cool, clear light in the evening. To people wandering in the desert or pasturing their flocks the moon appeared very wonderful. The changing shapes of the moon led these people to believe that it was a god showing himself in different forms. So we find that many ancient peoples kept every seventh day sacred at the time when the moon changed its form.

There is a remarkable hymn which the Babylonians must

have used in the worship of Sin, the moon-god, in his temple
at Ur. The hymn says that this god created the world and all
the things in it.

> Lord, thy divinity is like the distant heaven,
>   a broad sea full of fruitfulness,
> Who createth the land, foundeth the temples,
>   nameth their names,
> Father, who begetteth gods and man,
>   causeth dwellings to be set up,
>   and initiateth offerings;
>
> .   .   .   .
>
> In heaven—who is exalted?
>   Thou alone art exalted!
> On earth—who is exalted?
>   Thou alone art exalted!
>
> .   .   .   .
>
> Thy word bringeth forth truth and righteousness,
>   so that men speak the truth.
>
> .   .   .   .
>
> Look upon thy house! Look upon thy city!
>   Look upon Ur![1]

This old hymn makes us feel how much the Babylonians
loved and reverenced their god Sin, the moon-god. So it would
be most fitting to keep the Sabbath a holy day for his worship.

WORSHIP OF THE MOON BY THE HEBREWS

In a very old Hebrew law referring to the new moon we
read:

In the beginnings of your months, ye shall blow the trumpets
over your burnt-offerings, and over the sacrifices of your peace-
offerings. (Numbers 10:10)

The Hebrews kept this Sabbath day for hundreds of years
and held it sacred like their neighbors. Long after they
changed to the worship of Yahweh they began to think of it
as a day for the worship of God.

[1] Breasted, James H., *The Dawn of Conscience*, pp. 339, 340.

While some of the Jews were exiles in foreign lands, their leaders encouraged them to worship the Lord on the Sabbath. An unknown writer promises the Jews that they may become a great people if they properly keep the Sabbath and cease from all work, all pleasure, and idle talk and will delight themselves in God.

> If you refrain from doing your own business
>   upon the sabbath, on my sacred day,
> and hold the sabbath a delight,
>   and the Eternal's sacred day an honour,
> not following your own wonted round,
>   not doing business, and not talking idly,
> then you shall have delight in the Eternal's favour,
>   for he will let you hold the land in triumph,
> enjoying your father Jacob's heritage:
>   so the Eternal himself promises.[2]
>   (Isaiah 58:13, 14)

It took many hundreds of years before the Hebrews began to doubt the value of some of their ceremonies and the feast of the new moons. Here is what Isaiah believed that Yahweh said to the Hebrews:

> Your new moons and your appointed feasts my
>   soul hateth; they are trouble unto me.
>   (Isaiah 1:14)

Instead of such ceremonies, God seems to say to the Hebrews:

> Put away the evil of your doings from before
> mine eyes; cease to do evil; learn to do well;
> seek justice, relieve the oppressed.
>   (Isaiah 1:16, 17)

There was written a fourth law in the late Ten Commandments telling the Jews to keep the Sabbath holy.

> Remember the sabbath day, to keep it holy.
> Six days shalt thou labour and do all thy work:

[2] The Moffatt translation.

> But the seventh day is the sabbath of the Lord
> thy God: in it thou shalt not do any work, thou,
> nor thy son, nor thy daughter, thy man-servant,
> nor thy maid-servant, nor thy cattle, nor thy
> stranger that is within thy gates.
>   (Exodus 20:8-11)

The Sabbath day became a day sacred for the worship of Yahweh. All over the world the Jews may be seen going to their synagogues on Friday night and Saturday morning. Sometimes they go on Saturday afternoon for quiet talks and to study about "The Sayings of the Fathers."

A HEBREW WRITER EXPLAINS THE ORIGIN OF THE SABBATH

As the Hebrews gave up their belief in many spirits and became devoted to Yahweh, and finally to one God, they found a new reason for keeping the Sabbath a holy day for God. A beautiful poem may be found in the first chapter of Genesis in the Old Testament explaining the Jewish reason for keeping the Sabbath a holy day.

The priest tells the Jews how God made different parts of the earth and then created plants, animals and men to live on it. All of this work was done in six days. The priest closes his poem by telling how the Sabbath originated:

> God rested on the seventh day from all His work
> which He had made, and God blessed the seventh
> day and hallowed it.   (Genesis 2:2, 3)

SABBATH IN HEBREW HOMES

There are very beautiful services in Jewish homes on their Sabbath. After the father returns from the synagogue, he blesses the children and prays that each one shall become a noble Jew. Then the mother lights candles and blesses the lights and the father pronounces a Jewish benediction over the meal. This meal is a sort of festival. Psalms and songs are often sung.

There is a lovely old story that two angels always enter the Jewish home upon Sabbath eve and stand behind the master of the house when he returns from the synagogue. One angel is evil and dark; the other is beautiful and kind. If the home is disorderly and unprepared for the Sabbath feast, the bad angel says, "May all this man's Sabbaths be like this," and the good angel is forced to say a sad "Amen."

Let us imagine the house is clean, the candles lighted, the table set for the Friday evening feast; the wife is ready to welcome her husband home, and he greets her with Solomon's words concerning a good woman (Proverbs 31:10-12, 28-30):

Who can find a virtuous woman? for her price is far above rubies.
The heart of her husband doth safely trust in her, so that he shall
    have no need of spoil.
She will do him good and not evil all the days of her life."

.   .   .   .   .   .

Her children arise up, and call her blessed; her husband also, and
he praiseth her.
Many daughters have done virtuously, but thou excellest them all.
Favour is deceitful, and beauty is vain; but a woman that feareth
    the Lord, she shall be praised.

Then the good angel happily exclaims, "May all this man's Sabbaths be like this," and the bad angel is forced to answer, "Amen." It is only an old Jewish parable, but it shows us that the Jews believe that they must prepare very carefully for the Sabbath Day if they wish it to be a blessing to them. For thousands of years the Jews have kept this day for worship and to gain for themselves courage to live in the midst of people who have often been unfriendly to them.

Jewish home customs with their reverence and worship, have not greatly changed through the years. The play which follows shows how the Jews observe the Sabbath in their homes.

Shabbas Cheer

Characters: Father, Mother, Four Children, Two Boys, Two Girls, Man Guest.
Setting: *Sabbath table set.*
Mother (*lighting candles and praying*): Blessed art thou, O Lord our God, King of the universe, who hast sanctified us by thy commandments and hast commanded us to kindle the Sabbath lights.
First Girl: Mother, how lovely the Shabbas is. It always makes me feel like being good and having company.
Mother: Yes, dear. It is a lovely Jewish custom. "Remember the sabbath day . . ."
Second Girl: Oh, I know the whole commandment. It says: "Remember the sabbath day, to keep it holy. Six days shalt thou labor, and do all thy work; but the seventh day is a sabbath unto the Lord thy God. In it thou shalt not do any manner of work, thou, nor thy son, nor thy daughter, nor thy man-servant, nor thy maid-servant, nor thy cattle, nor the stranger that is within thy gates; for in six days the Lord made heaven and earth, the sea, and all that in them is, and rested on the seventh day; wherefore the Lord blessed the sabbath day, and hallowed it."
Mother: Good.
First Girl: I think we are very lucky to have Shabbas celebrated by father and you for us children, because it is just like getting an extra birthday party every week. Besides, Joyzelle told me that she was sorry that they never had Shabbas in her home. Her mother only lights candles when they have a bridge party.
Mother: It is too bad. What little children see in the home they will always remember when they grow up.
Second Girl: Hurrah, I hear them coming home from Shule.
(*Enter* Father, Man Guest *and* Two Boys.)
All: Good Shabbas.

ANSWER: Good Shabbas.

FATHER: Mother dear, let me introduce our Shabbas guest, Mr. Cohen.

MOTHER: Welcome to our house, Mr. Cohen.

GUEST: Thank you.

(*All take off their things and come to the table.*)

GUEST: How beautiful it is in here! Shabbas takes away all troubles from the Jew.

FIRST BOY: The rabbi says that Shabbas is like a beautiful bride.

SECOND BOY: My teacher in Sunday School says that's why the Jews must always welcome her with lights and songs and prayer.

FATHER (*laying his hands on the heads of the boys*): God make thee as Ephraim and Manasseh.

MOTHER (*laying her hands on the heads of the girls*): God make thee as Sarah, Rebekah, Rachel, and Leah.

FATHER: Good, now we will begin with Kisdush: "And it was evening and it was morning—the sixth day. . . . And the heaven and the earth were finished and all their host. And on the seventh day God had finished his work which he had made; and he rested on the seventh day from all his work which he had made. And God blessed the seventh day, and he hallowed it, because he rested thereon from all his work which God had created and made. . . . Blessed art thou, O Lord our God, King of the universe, who createst the fruit of the vine."

ALL: Amen.

FATHER: Mr. Cohen, will you honor us by saying grace?

GUEST: Gladly.

ALL: Praise be to thee, O Lord our God, who bringest forth bread from the ground.

(*All sit and are served with food.*)

FIRST BOY: That chale is some chale. No one makes it like mother.

SECOND BOY: Oh, boy, me for that fish!

FIRST GIRL: And wait for the zimmis!

GUEST: There is nothing like a good old-fashioned Yiddish Friday night meal to cheer one up.

(*At the end of the meal.*)

ALL: We thank thee, O God, for the gifts of thy bounty which we have enjoyed at this table. As thou hast provided for us till now, so mayest thou sustain us throughout our lives. Thy kindness endureth forever. Praise be to thee, O God, who sustainest the world in kindness. Amen.

FATHER: Now let us sing our Zmiros and rejoice.

HYMN:

HOLY SABBATH REST[3]

Allegro moderato   *Translated from German Hamburg Temple Hymnal*

Holy Sabbath rest! Pious lips thy advent hail;
With thee God His love hath sent,
Mind and heart of man to guard,
And to lead him heavenward.

Holy Sabbath joy! Oh! our yearning soul inspire;
Warm us with the heavenly fire,
That in sacred hymns of praise
We to God our hearts upraise.

Father Everlasting! From thy holy throne of grace
To thy children turn thy face:
Bless this day—preferred by Thee—
Emblem of eternity.

THE CHRISTIAN SUNDAY

Christians keep Sunday as their holy day. This came about after Jesus had died because his friends and followers chose the day after the Sabbath to meet for worship and to remember

[3] Music in *Pilgrim Elementary Teacher,* January, 1935, p. 8.

him. Gradually Sunday became the Christians' holy day and they no longer met on Saturday.

There have always been many problems among Christians about the best way to use Sunday. Customs become fixed and people observe them without thinking about their important meaning. Until recent years in Scotland no one dared to go for a walk on Sunday. It was forbidden to travel on that day even to help someone in need.

Jesus was severely criticized when he helped a sick man on the Jewish Sabbath day. But he answered by saying: "It is lawful to do good on the Sabbath day" (Matthew 12:12).

Once Jesus was going on the Sabbath day through the grainfields; and his disciples began . . . to pluck the ears. And the Pharisees said unto him, Behold why do they on the Sabbath day that which is not lawful? . . . And he said unto them, "The Sabbath was made for man, and not man for the Sabbath." (Mark 22: 23, 24, 28)

Many thoughtful people today believe that the Christian's Sunday should be a time for worship and rest and for those activities which improve life for the rest of the week.

Something to Do

1. Make plans for completing any play or pictures which you are creating.
2. If you know any Jewish people, try to find out how they observe their Sabbath day. Ask them to tell you their reasons for observing that day. Read more about Jewish customs in *With Jewish Child in Home and Synagogue*, by Elma Levinger.
3. Why did Christians change from the Jewish Sabbath to the observance of Sunday?
4. Have you ever confused references to the Sabbath in the Old Testament with Sunday which Christians observe? Read Isaiah 58:13.
5. After the exile a priestly writer tried to explain the origins of the Sabbath. Read what he said in Genesis 1 to 2:3.
6. Find out from different people their opinions about the way to observe Sunday.
7. What do you think are the finest ways for people of your age to spend Sunday?

CHAPTER XXI: THE HOME OF THE DEAD

THE DEAD IN SHEOL

After a person had died, the Hebrews did not expect that he could be brought back, not even by praying to Yahweh (II Samuel 12:23). When Jacob was told by his sons that Joseph had been devoured by wild beasts, he believed that the spirit of the boy would wait for him in Sheol (Genesis 37:33-35). The Hebrew writers of our Old Testament speak very often of a place called Sheol. Here, they believed, the spirits of the dead lived. It was a shadowy place under the earth and little was known about it. In desert times, the Hebrews had no idea of a place called heaven.

THE GREEK IDEA OF THE PLACE OF THE DEAD

The ancient Greeks also believed that the spirits of the dead went to live beneath the earth in a quiet, shadowy place. Many stories were told of spirits returning to earth, especially when they had not been properly buried. Sometimes these spirits were called back by the living to help them. One time, Periander of Corinth asked advice of the spirit of his wife, but the story says that she refused to help him until he gave her some new clothes to wear in the lower world. Periander went to a great festival where all the ladies were dressed in their best garments. Periander ordered them to take off their fine dresses and burn them in his wife's honor because in this way the dresses could be sent to the lower world. After his wife received them she granted her husband's wishes.

ROMAN IDEAS OF THE DEAD

The Romans also believed that the ghosts of the dead lived underground. In order to keep these ghosts from harming the living people, much attention was given to pleasing them. Sometimes bowls of warm milk and goblets of sacred blood were offered to the dead at the funeral in order to put the spirit at rest. A Roman father burned the playthings and pets of his son at the funeral in order that these things might go with him in the underworld.

Even Christians in Roman times thought that the dead needed food. It is said that the Christian mother of Augustine used to place cakes and bread and wine at the shrines of Christians who had been killed.

The Egyptians long ago imagined that the sky was the body of a woman bending over the earth-god, Keb, and that Shu, the god of the air, supported her.

RESURRECTION FROM THE DEAD

Palestine never seemed to be free from invaders and conquerors. About 332 B.C. the famous Greek ruler, Alexander the Great, invaded the land. At this time he was bringing most of the whole civilized world under Greek control. An old story tells us that the high priest of Jerusalem put on his most beautiful robes and went out to welcome Alexander. Probably the Jews had learned that it was useless to oppose him, so they welcomed him. Greek civilization surrounded them; Greek temples, theatres, and gymnasia were built in many towns and Greek ideas and customs began to be mixed with Jewish ones.

All was well until a stubborn ruler, Antiochus Epiphanes

(175 B.C.) arose and tried to crush all Jewish customs and ideas. He wanted to make Palestine entirely Greek. Greek altars were put up and Jews were ordered to sacrifice to Greek gods.

They shed innocent blood on every side of the sanctuary, and defiled the sanctuary. And the inhabitants of Jerusalem fled because of them. . . . Her feasts were turned into mourning, her sabbaths into reproach, her honor into contempt. (I Maccabees 1:37-39)

Faithful Jews were horrified, especially when Antiochus set up an altar to Zeus in the sacred Jewish temple of Jerusalem and offered swine upon it.

And many in Israel were fully resolved and confirmed in themselves not to eat unclean things. And they chose to die that they might not be defiled with the meats, and that they might not profane the holy covenant: and they died. (I Maccabees 1:62, 63)

Some Jews tried to drive out these enemies of their religion. This angered Antiochus and made him even more cruel. In the midst of such terrible suffering and persecution, a faithful Jew wrote the Book of Daniel to encourage his people to be true to their God and to trust Him to care for them. It is a difficult book for us to understand because he uses visions and symbols to teach his ideas.[1]

During these dark days people asked: Will those who have been killed ever have a share in the future when Israel is powerful and has her own ruler? Daniel said,

Many of them that sleep in the dust of the earth shall awake, some to everlasting life, and some to shame and everlasting contempt. (Daniel 12:2)

This is the first important saying in the Old Testament about the resurrection of the dead. Those faithful to God

[1] When Daniel refers to Babylon, he speaks of it as a lion; Media is like a bear; Persia is like a leopard; Greece is a terrible and powerful beast; Antiochus is a little horn. See Daniel 7:4-8.

shall be raised to eternal life while the wicked shall be punished.

In the Book of Enoch which was written about the same time we read, "In those days the earth will also give back those who are treasured up within it" (Enoch 51:1).[2]

The Jews were told that after the dead had come to life, there would be a Judgment Day when their deeds would be examined and judged. The righteous would be made happy either on the earth or in the heavens, while the wicked would be punished most terribly.

I looked and turned to another part of the earth and saw a deep valley with burning fire. And they brought the kings and the mighty and put them into this deep valley (Enoch 54:1, 2).

The writer of Enoch believed that there were spirits in the world to take charge of things. He referred to a spirit of the thunder and lightning and to a spirit of the sea. This is different from the desert ideas of the Hebrews because now the Hebrews knew that there is but one God and they were eager to learn how He works in the world.

BELIEFS IN THE TIME OF JESUS

Greek and Roman ideas

In the time of Jesus, both Greeks and Romans believed that heaven was a place above the stars where the gods and their messengers lived. When good people died, their spirits went to live with the gods in heaven.

A lower world received the spirits of evil people. Sometimes ordinary people were sent to it, in order to be purified and made ready to go up to heaven later on. It was a place where wicked people were tortured and punished in awful ways. Heaven was believed to be a beautiful place where people were very happy.

[2] In the days of persecution, a special class of books was written to keep alive the faith of the Jews. These have been called "apocalyptic" books. Apocalyptic comes from a Greek word meaning to uncover. The books uncovered the future. One of these books is called the Book of Enoch.

Jewish ideas in Jesus' time

Now the Jews, as they were called in Jesus' time, did not think as the Greeks and Romans did about the spirits of the dead. The Jews of this time thought that all spirits first went to the underworld. There they had to wait until God called all the dead to a Day of Judgment. Then the bodies of the dead would come to life. On that day the good people would be sent to paradise and happiness, and the wicked sent to a place of punishment and torture.

THE FOLLOWERS OF JESUS LOOKED FOR HIS RETURN

For a long time after Jesus had died, his followers preached that the end of the world would soon come and Jesus would return. When this happened, the spirits of the dead would come back to their old bodies and the good would be rewarded and the evil punished.

Perhaps you may know some people today who have the same ideas. For hundreds of years certain people have been saying that God was coming with His angels out of the heaven to judge people on earth and to separate the good from the evil people. Many times, these people have set dates for this to happen but God has never come in this way.

THE EARLY CHRISTIANS CHANGED THEIR IDEAS ABOUT JESUS' RETURN

After the early Christians had waited and the world did not come to an end and Jesus did not return, they began to change their beliefs. Instead of thinking that all the spirits of the dead lived in Sheol where they awaited a Day of Judgment, these Christians were influenced by some new ideas from such great Romans as Seneca and Plutarch. These men said that all good people were sent at once to live in paradise above the earth and in the sky; all sinners went under the earth to a place of endless punishment. So in the teaching of the Chris-

tians the ancient Sheol of the Hebrews became the home of
the wicked.

THE SPIRITS OR GODS ARE VERY NEAR

In the long past, we have seen how man has explained life
and mysterious things in the world as the work of spirits. Later
the Jews came to think of heaven as the home of God. Here He
was surrounded by His angels and so it is not surprising that
the Jews looked upon these heavenly beings as God's messengers making visits to the earth and doing things to living
people.

In the very old stories of the Hebrews in the Bible, God is
reported as visiting people and acting like a man. One story
tells of Him visiting the Garden of Eden to talk with Adam
and Eve (Genesis 3:8ff). Often Yahweh seems to have appeared to people as an angel.[3] We read of Him speaking to
Abraham (Genesis 17:1ff) and appearing to Isaac (Genesis
26:6). It is said that Jacob met God face to face and wrestled
with Him (Genesis 32:30, 48:31). Four chief men of Israel:
Moses, Aaron, Nadab, and Abihu, with seventy elders, came
before God in person. They ate and drank in his presence
(Exodus 24:9-11). Solomon met God face to face (I Kings
3:5, 9:2).

It was not until after some of the Hebrews had been carried
away as captives to live in foreign lands that they tended to
think of angels as distinct from Yahweh. In the time of Jesus,
ghosts, spirits, and angels were much talked about. We find
many references to angels in the stories written about Jesus in
our New Testament. They say that angels appeared at his
tomb and that an angel announced his birth to his parents.
An angelic choir sang the glad tidings on his birthday to some
shepherds in the fields. The Jews like other people in many
parts of the world have often explained unusual events as the

[3] References to angels or Yahweh: Genesis 16:7; Judges 6:11, 21-23; Exodus 3:2.
The Hebrew word mal'ak meant angel or messenger.

work of angels that were associated with God. Though people in Palestine have changed the name of their religion at times, you will still find people in the villages out in the country believing in spirits and angels. Try to think of all the pictures of Jesus which you have seen with angels in them. Some artists and church people have continued to believe in angels until the present day.

KNOWLEDGE CHANGES MAN'S IDEAS

A Child's Thought of God

They say that God lives very high!
    But if you look above the pines,
You cannot see our God. And why?

And if you dig down in the mines,
    You never see Him in the gold,
Though from Him all that's glory shines.

God is so good, He wears a fold
    Of heaven, and earth across His face—
Like secrets kept, for love, untold.

But still I feel that His embrace
    Slides down, by thrills, through all things made,
Through sight and sound of every place:

As if my tender mother laid
    On my shut lids, her kisses' pressure,
Half-waking me at night; and said,
    "Who kissed you through the dark, dear guesser?"
                        —Elizabeth Barrett Browning

Now we must remember that in the far-off days there were no giant telescopes to help the people learn how enormous the universe really is and how many millions of miles away the stars and planets are. In those days, no one had travelled around the earth to learn that it is round or ascended up above the clouds in an aeroplane. This lack of knowledge of the universe led to many primitive explanations of it.

But it is interesting to discover that Jews, Christians and other people have changed their religious beliefs from time to time, as they have found new explanations of the mysteries in the world around them. As they have learned about the sky above and the earth beneath, they have changed their ideas about heaven and Sheol and about angels and spirits. Just so have ideas about God also changed. Of course, there are some people today, who still hold to the ancient ideas about spirits and angels. But it is important to remember that these ideas of spirits and angels of heaven and of hell are borrowed from the long ago before people understood life and the universe as we do now.

Many Christians today are coming to think of God and of life and death in ways that seem to be consistent with the discoveries of science. As farmers have discovered the processes of storms and of drought or the science of agriculture they no longer turn to spirits to help them. Sick people no longer explain illness as the work of spirits. Doctors are learning the causes of illness and to apply proper remedies.

With the discoveries of science, man is no longer contented to explain things as the Hebrews and other ancient peoples tried to do thousands of years ago. The more we learn about the universe the greater and more wonderful it seems. Ancient peoples never dreamed of some of the marvels we are coming to know about today. Often these discoveries help us to form truer and nobler ideas of God and of the way He works in the world. Instead of spirits and magic, we are thinking of God working in orderly ways, and of the need for people to learn these ways and to co-operate with them.

We are learning to think of God as the spirit of goodness and of love which dwells within all people and in all of life, making it possible for people to grow nobler and finer. As man learns about the laws of the universe he has to learn to co-operate with them for the good of all people. There is great danger that he will forget about the ways of God and use his discoveries to destroy other people. Lindbergh in 1936 warned people that the aeroplane may be used in wars to destroy our cities, our art, and our civilization. Yet aeroplanes may be a great benefit. Knowledge of germs is useful to prevent disease, yet this knowledge may be used in wars to destroy health and life. Inventors give us wonderful machines that save labor, yet people may use them to make money for themselves and fail to provide enough pay or enough work to care for the needs of working people.

So as man gives up his belief in magic, in spirits and in many gods, it is very necessary that he come to find a truer idea of a God who works in this vast universe as we know it today. People are finding Him in love, in friendliness, in justice, in truth, in sacrifice, and in brotherhood. A few of the Hebrew prophets, some of the greatest teachers in other religions, many of our great Jewish and Christian teachers, particularly Jesus, have understood this. Tolstoi once said, "Where love is there God is." Man must learn to work with God in this orderly universe and he must learn how to express God's spirit in all of his actions. Goodness has power to grow and perhaps it is that part of people that lives forever.

Something to Do

1. Find out from several people what ideas they have about life after the death of the body. Compare these ideas with different ones found among ancient peoples.
2. Read II Samuel 12:22, 23 to see what the ancient Hebrews believed about bringing the dead back.
3. Read Genesis 37:33-35. What did this writer think happened to the dead Joseph?
4. What ideas about the dead did you find in Egypt? Read again Chapter V.
5. When did Jewish writers begin to speak about the resurrection of the dead? Read more about the book of Daniel at the close of Chapter XXV.
6. How did the Jews differ in their thinking from the Greeks and Romans regarding the dead?

7. What changes in belief about the dead grew among Christians when Jesus did not return as they had expected?

8. Perhaps you have found varied ideas among people today about what happens after death. Try to think of what happens to the good deeds of people even after their death. Try to trace their effect for awhile. Try to trace the effect of Jesus. If God is a living Spirit could there be any connection between such a God and the ongoing power of goodness?

CHAPTER XXII: A DARING DREAM

A young man, long ago, had a daring dream for the people of his land. The Romans governed his little country of Palestine. For hundreds of years the Jews had longed for a time to come when they would be free from oppression and have their beloved country for themselves. The young man heard them talking about armies, battles, palaces in Jerusalem, and kingdoms.

When he went to his synagogue he listened to the teachings of great Jewish leaders, read from the Old Testament, which was his Bible. He heard Jews talking excitedly about God sending them a leader in some wonderful way to be their king and to rule in Jerusalem.

The more he thought about the sufferings of his people and about their plans the more clearly he seemed to hear God asking him to become their leader and to build this new kingdom.

He was no longer needed at home. After his father Joseph had died, this young man had carried on his carpentry business and faithfully cared for the family. His four brothers and two sisters were growing up and able to care for the mother. He was past thirty years of age and the time had come to carry out his dream.

In order to think of his plans more carefully he went away to a desert place where he could be alone to think with God about his great dream. He wondered about the very best way to build this new kingdom for the Jews. How could he get people to listen to him?

One plan that tempted him was to do something startling, something miraculous like casting himself down from the top of the temple, and calling on angels to protect him. This would attract people's attention to his power. But after many days of

careful thinking and praying, he felt certain that God's kingdom could never be built by signs and wonders. So he cast
aside all suggestions of ways of magic.

During the years he had spent quietly at home he had been
noticing the way other people lived. He saw haughty rich people acting as if they were superior to the common people. He
saw people in the market places and in positions of power
cheating and oppressing the poor. He noticed that religious
leaders were sometimes very proud and often forgot to do good
to their neighbors.

He thought more and more about God. The grass of the
field, the red and purple anemones, and the birds of the air, all
seemed to speak to him of God's goodness and of His care
which was all around him. He came to believe that God was
like a loving father, surrounding men, women and children
with love.

So he dreamed of another kind of kingdom. In it men and
women would love each other so much that they would not
cheat, or be haughty or cruel. They would love people of all
races and of all nations. He thought about this nobler way of
living so much that he became certain that this must be his
work.

Instead of establishing powerful armies, or building great
palaces in Jerusalem, or becoming a popular hero, or using
magical deeds to build a kingdom, he decided to go about
living the way of love and teaching this great way to others.
His decision took enormous courage because the people did
not expect such a leader and many would not be pleased to
change their ways of living. But his dream of God's kingdom
had made him certain that this was the only kind of kingdom
that would help his people or endure.

After his desert experience he began talking to common
folk about God and about the ways of love. He told them how
to make others happy. He taught them to become sorry for
wrong deeds, to be kind, eager to help others, unselfish,

humble, forgiving, and to be willing to endure hard things in order to do good. He told them how important it was to overcome hatred and other evil thoughts and to think loving thoughts of others, even one's enemies. He spoke so earnestly and so simply that people were glad to hear him.

Often he spoke near the Lake of Galilee. Sometimes he would get into a boat and push out just far enough for the crowds on the shore to see and hear him easily. At other times he climbed up the slopes of a hillside and spoke to the people seated around him on the grass.

In order to spread ideas about his kingdom of love, this young man called some simple fishermen to leave their fishing and to join him in his work. He even succeeded in winning Matthew, a tax collector to join him. Probably Matthew had made much money through collecting taxes from the people, but the young man with his dream had helped him to see a nobler way of living. Finally he had gathered twelve men around him to become his special followers.

He often took them with him when he spoke to the people and always tried to help them to understand his dreams for the kingdom of love. They became very devoted to their leader. But it was very difficult for them to give up their idea of a powerful king in Jerusalem reigning over the Jews.

More and more, people came out to hear him. People waited along the roadside to see him or to have him touch them hoping that he would heal their diseases.

Once some mothers brought their children so that he might touch them. The young men whom he had called to follow him tried to push the children away but the teacher said: "Let the little children come unto me and forbid them not." Then he took some of the children up in his arms and blessed them.

One day he set out over the hills to his home town at Nazareth. Stories of his teaching and healing had reached the people there and they were excited to see him. On the Sabbath day he was invited to read in the synagogue from his Bible, which is our Old Testament. Then he told the people that he was called to do the things for God that he had been reading about. But he said, "You cannot see me do these wonderful things unless you have faith in me."

The people knew that he had been only a carpenter and it made them very angry to have him say that he was called of God to build a kingdom of love. So they tried to push him over the rocky cliffs. All at once it seemed as though his friends had become his enemies. Because he believed so much in the power of love, he did not strike back or become angry, and the people must have felt his noble courage, for it is said that he slipped away unharmed.

He went on teaching beside the Lake of Galilee, on the hillsides, and in the towns, and crowds of people came to hear him. This made some of the religious leaders, who were called Pharisees, afraid of his power. They did not always like his teachings, especially when he did not obey all of the old Jewish religious laws. He believed that it was more important to help people, to be good neighbors, and to show love for people, than it was to obey many of these old laws. Sometimes he criticized these Pharisees. So it is not surprising that they became angry with him and wanted to get rid of him.

It was nearing the time for the Jews to go up to Jerusalem to celebrate a great religious service called the Passover. The young teacher thought this would be the best possible chance to reach people with his teaching and to help the kingdom of love to grow.

To make such a trip was a dangerous thing to do. The Pharisees of his own country would be there and they would surely oppose him. Then there were the powerful leaders in the great temple called Sadducees who would be suspicious of this new teaching and fearful lest he lead the people to make trouble.

He faced all of these dangers. But he believed so firmly that he must lead his people to build God's kingdom of love that dangers to himself did not matter. With high courage he went.

He found people interested in hearing him. Sometimes they asked questions. They brought their troubles to him for advice. Often he talked to the people along the way and told them many beautiful stories which helped them to understand about God and his kingdom.

When he and his young followers came to Jericho, there was such a crowd that a taxgatherer named Zaccheus climbed up into a tree to see the famous teacher. Seeing his eager face, he said, "Zaccheus, come down quickly! for I must stay at your house today." Zaccheus came down and welcomed him gladly. But some of the people standing by criticized him and said, "He has gone to stay with an irreligious man." But Zaccheus must have been greatly impressed by the teacher's loving spirit, for he said to him, "See, Master! I will give half my property to the poor, and if I have cheated anyone of anything, I will pay him four times as much."

The young teacher's dreams were beginning to come true. His love for the poor, for taxgatherers who cheated, and for others who had done wrong, seemed to have enormous power in changing them. But strangely enough his friendliness for such people brought him increasing criticism from some of the religious leaders.

Each morning he walked to Jerusalem and spent the day at the temple and in the evening returned to the nearby village of Bethany. One day he decided to ride into Jerusalem on a donkey. He wanted to make clear to the people that he was not coming as a warrior king, but in a peaceful way. Many people who had heard him speak came out to greet him. In a short time there was a crowd surrounding him. Palm branches were waved, garments were spread in his path and the air rang with the shouts of "Hosanna, Hosanna."

When the leaders in Jerusalem saw all of this enthusiasm for him, they decided that such popularity would be dangerous. Nevertheless, on his arrival at the great temple of Herod, he began speaking about a nobler religion. He even reproved the leaders for their proud ways and for their treatment of the poor and less fortunate people.

This made some of the Pharisees and Sadducees very angry. So a few of them decided that this teacher was a dangerous person and must be put to death at once. Since he had so many followers they knew that it must be done quietly.

But the young teacher with his great dream kept right on teaching. He knew that he was in grave danger, but he felt that God's plans must be carried out.

One night he met with his twelve disciples at a religious feast called the Passover. He spoke very earnestly to them about his dream for the kingdom of love. He tried to encourage them to go on with his plans, and to do it all in a loving spirit even if they were made to suffer and were persecuted. He told them that this kingdom must be built in the hearts of people.

After singing a hymn, the young man and his disciples left Jerusalem and went over to the Mount of Olives. The teacher went apart under some olive trees to pray. Judas, who was one of the twelve, was missing. The other disciples were sleeping and resting. So the young teacher seemed all alone. He began to pray earnestly for God to help him. It took such courage to carry out his plans. Enemies were beginning to plot against him. How could he carry out his dream? All would be lost if he left Jerusalem now. Perhaps if he were put to death for his dream, it would make more people understand the kingdom of love.

Just as he had made this great decision to remain loyal to his dream, he saw some soldiers coming through the trees with lighted torches. He became very calm. He was not afraid. But he must have been very, very sad, when he saw that Judas, one of his twelve disciples, was leading the soldiers to arrest him! Judas had betrayed him. No one knows why.

Because some of the leaders in Jerusalem could not understand about his kingdom of love, they put him to death in a very cruel way. But at the time when he was suffering most terribly, he still thought of the people who could not understand, and prayed the noblest prayer of all time, "Father, forgive them for they know not what they do."

This young teacher was Jesus. At first it seemed as though his dream had failed. But gradually his disciples began to comprehend what he had said about the way of love. They realized that people had killed only the body of their great leader Jesus, but that his spirit was alive. Love could not be killed. Some of these friends of Jesus had to suffer many things, too, but they carried on Jesus' spirit of love so much that even their enemies said, "Behold, how these Christians love one another." Many people listened to their teaching and finally churches were formed for those who wanted to help.

For nearly two thousand years Jesus' teachings have spread and there have been faithful people in the churches even until the present time who have tried to carry out his daring dream of a kingdom of love, believing that God is in and on the side of all love and goodness in the world.

> Give us, O God, the strength to build
> The city that hath stood
> Too long a dream, whose laws are love,
> Whose ways are brotherhood,
> And where the sun that shineth is
> God's grace for human good.
> —Walter Russell Bowie

Something to Do

1. What should be added to your pictures or to your play from this chapter?
2. Read all the Gospel of Mark in the New Testament at one sitting to see what that writer long ago thought was important to record about Jesus. Try to read a thrilling play about Jesus, *Family Portrait,* by Coffee and Cowen.
3. What things did Jesus say or do that you think are nobler than the religious practices or ideas before the exile?
4. Make a poster and list in one column primitive ideas of God

and in another, noble ideas of God which you have discovered in this course.

5. If God supports all goodness and dwells in people (I John 4:7, 12, 18; John 4:24) how would you answer the following questions?

   (a) Where will you be able to find clearest evidences of God?

   (b) How would this help you to stand for the hard right against an easy wrong?

   (c) What would be the strongest relation to any enemy? (Read Luke 23:34.)

   (d) What should be the purpose of an employer: to accumulate money and power or to work for the best interest of those whom he employs?

   (e) A person says, "I would fail in my profession if I were to follow the teachings of Jesus."

CHAPTER XXIII: HOW WE LEARN ABOUT THE PAST

One of the greatest discoveries of ancient times was the art of writing. No single invention made by early people has helped more to make our life what it is today.

PICTURE WRITING

In the first writing objects were referred to by making pictures of them. Then words were made by groups of little pictures. For example, to write the word *day* a circle was drawn. This circle was the sun. A moon and a star were used to make the word *night*. In Egypt, there have been found a great many of these picture writings. The Egyptians were probably among the first people to write out their ideas. Some people think that theirs is the prettiest writing that has ever been known. It is called "hieroglyphic," which means "sacred carving."

The Egyptians were also the first people to make paper, and they used it long before other people had learned its practical use. Of course today we would think their books very clumsy if we compared them with our modern books.

To make a book in Egypt it was necessary to gather stems of a reed called papyrus, which grew in marshy places. This plant grew sometimes to a height of fifteen feet and had a stalk about six inches thick. After the outer covering of the stalk was removed, the inner part was separated into thin layers. These layers were laid out side by side and a thin gum spread over them. Then another layer was prepared in the same way and laid crosswise on the top of the first. This double sheet was put into a press, squeezed together, and dried.

Sheets of paper were not bound into a book but joined end-to-end as they were needed for writing. As parts of the book were finished, they were rolled up until it formed a big roll, sometimes many feet long. One of them in the British Museum measures 135 feet in length.

Papyrus grew on the banks of the river Nile.

By thickening water with a vegetable gum and adding soot to it, the Egyptians made ink. A pointed reed was used for a pen.

Many of the papyrus rolls were written to place in the tombs of the dead. Some of them are very beautiful and illustrated with delightful pictures in color to represent scenes of life in another world. Little did these writers think that, thousands of years after, scholars would dig up their writings and read them. But it is from these writings that we have learned so much about Egyptian religion. From these writings scholars have discovered that the Egyptians were beginning to think some of the noblest thoughts about God and about religion. These discoveries have taught us how much we owe to man's quest for God in the long past.

Writings that were to last a very long time were written or cut into stones. The stones of many of the Pharaohs (kings) were carved deep and clear in the hard granite of a great obelisk, or in the limestone of a temple wall. After the lines were cut in stone, they were filled in with different colored pastes so that the walls looked as if they were covered with finely colored tapestries. After thousand of years much of the color has disappeared. Still there are some temples and tombs where the color is almost as fresh as when it was laid on.

CLAY TABLETS

The Assyrians also took great pains to write down poems, proverbs, fairy stories, the deeds of their great men, and the

Libraries in Assyria and Babylonia contained clay tablets like these instead of books.

adventures of their heroes. These people developed another kind of writing. A lump of soft clay was molded into a tablet a few inches square. The writing was done with a sharp-pointed instrument called a stylus. It was used to press little v-shaped marks into the wet clay. These wedges were used to make words, then the tablet was baked in the sun. The tablets were kept in libraries much as we keep books today. For thirty centuries this kind of writing was used by people living along the Tigris and Euphrates rivers.

Scholars have learned to read the writing on the tombs and temples in Egypt and on the clay tablets in Assyria, and in this way have given us marvelous ideas of life in the days before the Hebrews had become more than primitive nomads.

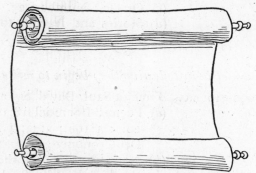

The Hebrew writings were written on scrolls.

PARCHMENT SCROLLS

When the Hebrews first began to write they probably made use of papyrus and then later discovered the use of parchment.

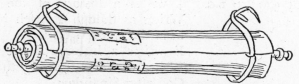

A scroll was the form of the Hebrew Bible.

Parchment was made by soaking sheepskin or goatskin so that the hair could be pulled out. The skin was stretched on a frame and dried. It was then scraped with a stone and rubbed until smooth. The Hebrews wrote on this and then rolled it into a scroll.

CHART V: *Order of Writing of the Hebrew Bible or Our Old Testament*

A

Stories, songs and proverbs while the Hebrews were nomads

1. Before 1000 B.C.   (a) War and March songs: Exodus 15: 21; 17:16; Numbers 21:27-30; 2: 17f.; Joshua 10:12f.; Judges 5.
(b) Proverbs, riddles, fables: I Samuel 24:13; Judges 14:14, 18; 9:7-15.
(c) Oracles: Numbers 23.
(d) Stories and legends told orally.

B

As the Hebrews settle in Palestine they begin to write their history

2. About 1000-910 B.C.   Time of Saul, David, Solomon.
(a) Poems: I Samuel 18:17; II Samuel 20:1; 1:19ff.; 3:33; I Kings 8:12f.; Deuteronomy 33.
(b) Narratives: story of the founding of the kingdom by Saul, David, and Solomon in parts of I and II Samuel and I Kings 1f.; parts of I Kings 3-11.

3. About 910-700 B.C.   Elijah stories: I Kings 17-19.
Elisha stories: II Kings 2-8, in part.

4. About 950-850 B.C.   J writes a history of the Hebrews. Writes as though Yahweh had always been the Hebrew God.

5. 750 B.C.   E writes a history of the Hebrews. Writes of Yahweh being the Hebrew God after Sinai days.

6. 748-735 B.C.   Amos speaks to Israel. Parts seem to belong to an unknown writer after the exile.

7. 745-735 B.C.   Hosea speaks to Israel. Parts seem to belong to unknown writers of the exile.

8.	738-700 B.C.	Isaiah speaks to Judah.
9.	700 B.C.	J and E histories are combined.
10.	626 B.C.	Jeremiah.
11.	621 B.C.	Deuteronomy published.
12.	620 B.C.	First edition of the Book of Kings.

C

After the Hebrew kingdom was destroyed and some Hebrews were taken into exile, belief in one God is stressed

13.	593-571 B.C.	Ezekiel. The Holiness Code (Leviticus 17-26). Isaiah 63:7 to 64:12; nobler laws. J, E, and D histories joined together in our first five books of the Bible.
14.	550 B.C.	Revision of I Kings and II Kings. D writes the stories of Joshua, Judges. An unknown writer writes Isaiah 40-55. He challenges the Jews to become God's missionaries to the world.
15.	500 B.C.	The Priest's Code is written: Isaiah 59: 15b; 63:6; 65:17-25; 66:7-14; 11:10 to 16:34f. Amos 9:8b-15; Genesis 1 to 2:4a. Jeremiah 3:14-18. Probably the Ten Commandments: Exodus 20.
16.	430 B.C.	Nehemiah and Ruth. Ezra 4:8-6; 18.
17.	400 B.C.	Joel. Isaiah 19:1-15; 23:1-14. Older parts of Proverbs; Job; Isaiah 24-27.
18.	300-200 B.C.	The Chronicles. Genesis 14. I Kings 13. Esther. Jonah. Isaiah 19:18-25.
19.	200 B.C.	Ecclesiastes.

20. 165-164 B.C.   Daniel.
                          Zechariah 12; 13:1-6; 14:9-11; 13:7-9.
                          Psalter completed.
                          The Old Testament completed.
                          Isaiah 33.

Something to Do

1. Make some posters illustrating ways we have learned from the past. Read *The World We Live In,* by Gertrude Hartman or *How the Present Came from the Past,* by M. E. Wells, to discover more about the way we have learned from the past.

2. Study Chart V in order to discover the way the Old Testament grew.

   (a) How does the order in the Chart differ from the arrangement in your Bible?

   (b) Compare Charts I and II with Chart V to discover how much history had passed before very much was written as we have it in our Old Testament.

   (c) Notice when Genesis 1 to 2:4a was written.

   (d) Notice the different dates for parts of Isaiah.

3. What confusion could arise for readers who do not know the period when parts of a book were written?

CHAPTER XXIV: HOW THE HEBREWS WROTE THEIR BOOKS

After the Hebrews became united as a nation and were settled in Canaan, it seems perfectly natural that they should have begun to keep records of their history. Other countries such as Egypt kept such records and the Hebrews must have learned much from them and from the advanced civilization of the Canaanites into whose land they had come. Probably the Hebrews learned to write the language of Canaan. The Hebrew language is much like other Semitic languages found on ancient stones and tablets.

After their exile in Babylon, the Jews ceased to speak Hebrew and used a language called Aramaic. This was the language spoken in Syria, a country in the northern part of Palestine. The Hebrew language continued to be the written language and was regarded as sacred for religious writings.

DIFFICULTY IN UNDERSTANDING HEBREW HISTORY

The books in our Old Testament cover the story of a people during many hundreds of years. We have noticed again and again how the Hebrews changed and grew in some of their religious ideas. At times these changes in their thinking were written into new histories. Then later on these different histories were combined. For example, in the first book of our Old Testament, Genesis, we have the writings of some unknown authors whom we call J, E, and P, blended together. Two stories of the creation stand side by side. The later ideas of P come in the first chapter of Genesis and the primitive ideas of an earlier writer in the second chapter.

Of course when the writers put the works together and rearranged them they did not make footnotes to tell which writer had first written a certain part. So we have to depend upon scholars who can recognize the differences in the Hebrew language in which these books were first written. There are other differences too. But, because of these varied writings being combined in our Bible, we must understand that no one can commence at the beginning of the Bible and expect to find events in the order in which they were first written down. Even more important is it for readers of the Old Testament to know that the religious ideas and customs of the Hebrews are not to be found in the Bible in the order in which they grew and developed.

Compare what two writers in different periods say about the same event.

J writes (950 B.C.)	*P writes* (After 500 B.C.)
As for the Jebusites, the inhabitants of Jerusalem, the children of Judah could not drive them out. (Joshua 15:63)	And the children of Judah fought against Jerusalem and took it and smote it with the edge of the sword. (Judges 1:8)

Hebrew historians wrote for their own people, not for us today. They used history to teach their own religious ideas at a certain definite time, not merely to review past history. They did not hesitate to change older stories in order to express their own ideas. If this is carefully remembered, then people who read the Bible will come to understand why there are so many repetitions and why there are so many disagreements between events and ideas which are repeated in different parts of the Bible.

The Bible is a library of many books, written by many different authors on different occasions. To most of these writings, additions and changes were made by later writers.

The library of books in our Old Testament was probably a thousand years in its formation. It has become the most sacred of all books to the Jews. This same library is also sacred to Christians and to Muslims (those people all over the world who reverence Muhammed instead of Jesus).

STORYTELLERS INSTEAD OF STORYBOOKS

Egyptians, Babylonians, Hebrews and other people in the long past asked questions just as people do today. They wanted to know how the world began, about the creation of man and of life on the earth. They asked why there is suffering and why man has to work so hard. In their stories we find some of their answers to these questions. Probably the Hebrews heard many of these stories from the neighboring people around them: the Babylonians, the Egyptians, and the Canaanites. As they told them over and over for hundreds of years, quite naturally parts of the story were changed and new ideas began to be woven into them. Religious tales, originally told about the baalim of the Canaanites or the god Marduk of the Babylonians or other gods, began to be changed and told about the Hebrew God, Yahweh. How long this change had been going on we do not know, but it is fairly certain that stories were told for many centuries before they were written.

Probably the oldest parts in our Bible are some of the poems about war[1] and some of the proverbs, riddles and fables.[2] These battle songs are very cruel and barbaric and quite unlike the spirit of poems written hundreds of years later, but they show how primitive the people[3] were then and how people have progressed.

LAWS CHANGE AS THE HEBREWS DEVELOP

Another old part of our Bible is that containing some of the Hebrew laws. Often the later writers of these laws say that

[1] Very ancient war and march songs may be found in the following references: the song of Miriam (Exodus 15:21); eternal war with Amalek (Exodus 17:16); taunt song on the Amorites (Numbers 21:27-30); song of the well (Numbers 21:17f); song of Deborah (Judges 5).

[2] Jotham's fable (Judges 9:7-15).

[3] Alois Musil tells about Bedouin lore today in his book *The Manners and Customs of the Ruala Bedouins* (New York, 1928), p. 283f. Even today poems are recited in the camp; one remembers a part, someone remembers another part, and by helping each other they are completed, but always with changes.

Moses gave them to the Hebrews or that Yahweh gave them to Moses and that he then passed them on to the Hebrews.

Many scholars who have studied the Bible very carefully are convinced that Moses could not have given all these varied laws. The laws reveal different ways of living. Some are the very primitive laws of nomads. Others are for people settled down as farmers. Some are cruel. Others are noble and remind us of Jesus. Because the Hebrews thought of Moses somewhat as we do of George Washington they came to think that Moses gave them most of their laws. Since history was not written down during the hundreds of years the Hebrews lived in the desert, it was impossible to remember how and when all the customs and laws had started.

Many peoples have said that their laws were given to them by the gods. The Babylonians thought that their laws were given to their great ruler, Hammurabi, by the sun-god, Shamash. The Greeks likewise considered that they had received many of their laws from the gods. So we find the Hebrews teaching their children that Yahweh gave to Moses many of their laws.

Usually laws begin when there are problems to be decided. If the new rule or law seems sensible, then it is repeated. As the Hebrews left their desert life to live in Palestine with strange neighbors, new customs and new laws were needed. These Canaanitish neighbors were more civilized than the Hebrews. They had been learning many things from the Babylonians for centuries. Probably in this way the Hebrews also learned about Babylonian laws and customs.

LAWS MADE BY HAMMURABI

If you read the laws of the ancient Babylonian ruler called Hammurabi, you will discover that many laws of the Hebrews were much like his laws. This ancient code of laws has come down to us on a block of black stone once set up in a temple to Marduk in Babylon. Hammurabi lived about 2200 B.C. A few of his laws follow:

14. If a man steals the son of a man who is a minor, he shall be put to death.

15. If a man shall cut down a tree in a man's orchard without the consent of the owner, he shall pay one-half mana of silver. (These were date orchards.)

Here Hammurabi is receiving laws from the sun-god of Babylon. He says: "By the command of Shamash (the sun god), the great judge of heaven and earth, let righteousness go forth in the land."

195. If a son strikes his father, they shall cut off his hand.

200. If a man knocks out the tooth of a man of his own rank, they shall knock his tooth out.

233. If a builder builds a house for a man and does not make his work strong and a wall falls, that builder shall strengthen that wall at his own expense.

SOME HEBREW LAWS

In Exodus 21:1 to 22:17 there are Hebrew laws which resemble these old laws of Hammurabi. Just as Hammurabi was said to have received his code from Shamash, so we are told that the Hebrew code was given to Moses by Yahweh.

He that smites a man, so that he dies, shall surely be put to death. (Exodus 21:12)

And he that smites his father, or his mother, shall surely be put to death. (Exodus 21:15)

But if any harm follow, then thou shalt give life for life, eye for eye, tooth for tooth, burning for burning, wound for wound, stripe for stripe. (Exodus 21:23-25)

If thou meet thine enemy's ox or his ass going astray, thou shalt surely bring it back to him. Thou shalt not see the ass of him that hates thee lying under his burden, and forbear to help him; thou shalt surely help him. (Exodus 23:4, 5)

If we read some teachings that Jesus gave hundreds of years later, we can see how much progress the Jews had made by his time (Matthew 5:38-45). We find Jesus teaching people to love each other, even their enemies, rather than to take revenge or to try to get even with another.

In the most primitive days of the Hebrews they considered it necessary, when they were aroused to white heat against an enemy, to conquer and destroy him. They believed that this hatred was shared by their god and so this cruel massacre of an enemy,[4] became a sort of religious duty.

THE TEN COMMANDMENTS

Perhaps the Hebrew laws that you have heard most often mentioned are the Ten Commandments. If you should read the laws in the Old Testament more carefully you would find that there are many commandments, some of them much older than the Ten Commandments.

Since many writers at different periods in the history of the Hebrews wrote down laws, it is interesting to notice the changes which were made. Many of these laws are written as if they had been dictated by Yahweh to Moses. Probably the Hebrew writers believed that Moses was such a great leader that all important things in their religion came through him.

The oldest one of the codes of laws, said to have been given

[4] Read Joshua 6:21 and I Samuel 15:3-8.

by Yahweh to Moses, may be read in Exodus 34:14-28. This is sometimes called "The Ten Commandments of J," because J was one of the earliest writers of Hebrew history. Scholars believe this to be a very old code of laws because it seems related to the needs of a wandering people.

"Ten Commandments of J" are something as follows:

1. Thou shalt worship no other god. [Yahweh seems to be a jealous god. The people still believed in many gods.]
2. Thou shalt make thee no molten gods.
3. The feast of the Passover thou shalt keep.
4. None shall appear before me empty-handed.
5. Six days thou shalt work, but on the seventh thou shalt rest.
6. Thou shalt observe the feast of ingathering.
7. Thou shalt not offer the blood of my sacrifice with leavened bread.
8. The fat of my sacrifice shall not remain until the morning.
9. The firstlings of thy flocks thou shalt bring unto Yahweh thy god.
10. Thou shalt not seethe a kid in his mother's milk.

Nearly all of these laws are concerned with the ritual of worship. This ritual was the chief concern of nomadic people in their worship. It seemed most important for people to be faithful to the special service of the gods. Probably Yahweh was the god of the mountain. Later Hebrews were taught to worship him alone because he was a jealous god. This idea about Yahweh grew among the Hebrews until finally they gave up their worship of all gods except one God of all people.

As the Hebrews settled in Palestine and became an agricultural people, new law codes were formed. Probably it was hundreds of years after the time of Moses, that the famous Ten Commandments, found in Exodus 20:3-17, developed. In order to impress upon the Hebrews the importance of these laws, the writer says:

And Mount Sinai, the whole of it smoked, because Yahweh descended upon it in fire; and the smoke thereof ascended as the smoke of a furnace, and the whole mount quaked greatly. And when the voice of the trumpet waxed louder and louder, Moses spake, and God answered him by a voice. (Exodus 19:18, 19)

Then follow the laws which this later writer says were given to Moses.

1. I, Yahweh am your god.
2. You shall have no other gods.
3. You shall not invoke the name of your god for evil.
4. Remember to keep the Sabbath holy.
5. Honor your father and mother.
6. You must not commit murder.
7. You must not commit adultery.
8. You must not steal.
9. You must not bear false witness.
10. You must not covet your neighbor's house.

If you compare these later laws with the earliest ones, you will notice in the second code that God seems to demand that his followers serve him through good conduct. In the oldest code Yahweh demanded offerings and special ceremonies of worship. When the Hebrew people came to think of their god requiring noble conduct, they had progressed a long way from their primitive worship in the desert.

Something to Do

1. What differences can you find between Genesis 2:4b-24, written by J and Genesis 1:1-2:4a, written by P several hundred years later. These two stories may be studied in parallel columns in Wallis' *God and the Social Process*, pages 315-317.
2. Compare the earlier law of D in Deuteronomy 14:21, with a law written by P after the exile, Leviticus 17:15, 16.
3. Read some of the oldest parts of the Bible and notice their ideas of God and of life:

Exodus 15:21	Numbers 21:27-30
Exodus 17:16	Numbers 21:17-19
Judges 5	Judges 9:7-15

4. Compare some of the earliest Hebrew laws with Jesus' teachings many hundreds of years later: I Samuel 15:3, 8; Exodus 21 and 23;

Joshua 6:21; Matthew 5:38-45. What differences do you find in ways of treating people?

5. What are the differences between the Ten Commandments of J in Exodus 34:14-28 and the later Ten Commandments in Exodus 20:3-17. There is another code in Deuteronomy 5:6-21. Notice what later writers had to say about sacrifices: Psalm 50:7-15; Psalm 51:16, 17, and Micah 6:6-8.

CHAPTER XXV: HOW THE HEBREWS WROTE THEIR BOOKS (*Continued*)

THE FIRST HEBREW HISTORY

It was after the Hebrews had begun to live a more settled life in Palestine that they felt the need of writing down their stories and the history of their past.

Scholars tell us that it was about 950 B.C. that some unknown writer, whom they call the Judean, gathered the various stories together and wrote the first history of the Hebrews. This history began with the time when the Hebrews first came into Canaan and continued until they were ruling the land. Some of it is in the Book of Genesis, but here it is combined with history written by later writers. Parts are also found in Exodus, Numbers, Joshua and Judges.

The Judean writer used stories to teach religion. He wanted the Hebrews to believe in one great god, a creator god, and a god who should be the only god of the Hebrews. Since Yahweh had done so much for them, the Judean taught that they must be faithful to this god. So, as he wrote their history, he stressed the need for the Hebrews to be loyal to Yahweh. He did not remind the people of their primitive worship of the ēlim of the desert or of the baalim in Canaan. He wrote as if they had always worshiped Yahweh.

E WRITES ANOTHER HISTORY OF THE HEBREWS

Nearly two hundred years later (750 B.C.) in the northern part of Palestine, a writer whom we shall call E wrote a history of the Hebrews that is in many ways quite similar to that written by the Judean or the J writer. A very noticeable difference is that E refers to God as Elohim while the Judean uses the word Yahweh. E begins his history with a story of

Abraham. There are often parts of the story of E that disagree with the story of J.

Many years after E's history was written, the two histories of J, E, and P were pieced together into one book much as we have it in our Bible now. We find that this combined story even included parts where the writers differed. Sometimes this joining together of writings makes it difficult for people today, who are not scholars, to understand parts of the Old Testament in our Bible.

E tells stories of pillars and trees. But to him they are merely memorials to his god, not the habitation of spirits. E believed that God dwelt in heaven and came down to earth or went up by a stairway, appearing as an angel.

E told his story of the Hebrews just as the Judean did, in order to teach them[1] his religious ideas. He was bitter in his opposition to other gods. He wanted the Hebrews to believe that they were a people guided and controlled by one god. E believed that Yahweh became the new god of the Hebrews while Moses was their leader in Midian. He did not seem to think that his people had ever worshiped Yahweh before this time and in this he was probably correct. For centuries the Hebrews very likely had worshiped the ēlim as other Semites around them had done.

One of the favorite stories of E is the beautiful one about Joseph which is recorded in Genesis and begins in Chapter 37.

THE PROPHETS WRITE BOOKS

Beliefs changed, as we can see in the writings of the prophets who came forth to tell the people about Yahweh. After men like Amos, Hosea, Isaiah, and Micah had spoken, their messages were written down. Some parts of their teachings may be found in our Old Testament. Later Jewish writers probably added whole chapters to such books as Amos, Hosea, and

[1] Joshua 24:14-24 shows how E used his story to persuade his people to put away other gods.

Isaiah. Though much of the original material still remains, we find that the loftier ideas of God and of religion were probably added to these writings after the exile. In the chart giving the dates of some of the Old Testament writings you will notice that different parts of the Book of Isaiah are written at different dates.

It was a slow process to change the Hebrews from their age-long customs of worshiping like other peoples around them. In 621 B.C. a new book of religious laws was published. Its name is Deuteronomy which means "repeated laws." Every possible suggestion was made to purify the Hebrew religion of its old customs and beliefs. Sacrifices and festivals, it was urged, should be carried out only in the temple at Jerusalem.

This writer whom we shall call D told the people to break down and to destroy all of their old altars, pillars and images. He felt that the worship of Yahweh had been hindered by contacts with the Canaanitish worship. Here are some of his words:

Ye shall destroy all the places wherein the nations that ye shall dispossess served their gods, upon the high mountains and upon the hills, and under every green tree: and ye shall break down their altars, and dash in pieces their pillars, and hew down their asherim; and ye shall burn with fire the graven images of their gods; and ye shall destroy their name out of that place. Ye shall not do so to Yahweh your God. (Deuteronomy 12:2-4)

D gave the Hebrews their famous Shema which all faithful Hebrews have repeated in their worship for centuries, even to the present day. Shema means "hear." It is the first word of this ancient law which is found in Deuteronomy 6:4-9. Jesus quoted a part of it as the first and most important commandment. It begins:

Hear, O Israel: Yahweh is our God, Yahweh alone; and thou shalt love Yahweh thy God with all thy heart, and with all thy soul, and with all thy might. (Deuteronomy 6:4)

About the time this new book of laws by D was completed, the Hebrew king, Josiah, tried to put them into practice. He destroyed many of the "high places," ancient altars, and sacred pillars and stones. The Passover and other festivals were celebrated only in Jerusalem according to the new law. The temple at Jerusalem was cleansed and made ready for the worship of Yahweh alone.

In order to make the many laws and rules in this great reform appeal to the Hebrews, we find that it reads as if Yahweh had given them to their great hero, Moses. Probably some of these laws were changed from those that had grown out of a much older law (Exodus 34).

Not all of these laws are noble ones. There remains in some of them a spirit of revenge, even though the reformers were working to get justice. In cases of wrongdoing they still said, "And thine eyes shall not pity; life for life, eye for eye, tooth for tooth, hand for hand, foot for foot" (Deuteronomy 19:21). The D writer believes that the Hebrews should destroy all of the Canaanites. He says, "Thou shalt not save anything alive that breatheth" (Deuteronomy 20:16, 17). The Hebrew religion had not yet accepted Jesus' ideas of love and forgiveness and peace. D believed that Yahweh was interested only in the Hebrews, so when they went to their wars they expected their god to help them to be victorious.

THE HOLINESS CODE

More than a hundred years later, while the Jewish leaders were in exile, this law of revenge was changed. The prophet Ezekiel taught that God would be the judge of people's sins. He and other Jewish leaders said that people were punished for their own sins. Nobody could be saved by the goodness of another.

Some of the exiles made a new law code called the "Holiness Code."[2] The noblest part of it is in great contrast to some of

[2] This code may be found in Leviticus 17-26. It was probably arranged sometime before 500 B.C.

the spirit of the Deuteronomic Code. In this later code God is becoming a God of justice and of goodness. The Holiness Code reminds us of Jesus when it says:

Thou shalt not hate thy brother in thy heart: thou shalt surely warn thy neighbor, and not incur sin because of him. Thou shalt not take vengeance nor bear any grudge against the children of thy people, but thou shalt love thy neighbor as thyself: I am Yahweh. (Leviticus 19:17, 18)

In these days after the exile the Old Testament writings begin to give higher teachings. The inner spirit as well as the outer deeds are considered important. Of course this writer of the Holiness Code was thinking more about love among the Jews than toward foreigners. It was still later on that a Jewish writer joined together this law of love for one's neighbor as equally important with the law to love God.[3] Jesus believed that the two ideas belonged together. He taught that true love for God required that one should love not only his neighbor but his enemies as well (Matthew 5:43-48, Luke 6:27-36).

Ezekiel tried to make changes in the Hebrew worship. In the Holiness Code the Jews were forbidden to kill their own animals for sacrifice as they had been doing for centuries. The new law demanded that priests should do it for them. The prophet Ezekiel emphasized that priests should hold positions of importance in the temple and should depend on the Levites to do the menial work. Hebrew worshipers were taught to do things for Yahweh in the temple instead of other places. Gradually Hebrew worship became very formal and separate from practical living. Priests began to teach that Yahweh's sacrifices and worship were holy or separate. In this way it was hoped to keep the worship of God apart from the worship of that of many other gods. Instead of the Hebrew people killing their own sacrifices as of old, now they had to be brought to the temple and prepared and offered by the priests.

[3] "Thou shalt love thy neighbor as thyself: I am Yahweh" (Leviticus 19:18). "Thou shalt love the stranger as thyself: I am Yahweh" (Leviticus 19:34). These two laws were united in a book called *The Testaments of the Twelve Patriarchs.*

From such teaching Jewish worship gradually became more and more elaborate. The work of Ezekiel and the new Holiness Code prepared the way for vast numbers of laws and ceremonies of worship that finally made the religion of the Jews almost a burden to them. By the time Jesus was teaching in Palestine, he saw some religious leaders paying so much attention to these laws and to the temple worship that they forgot to be kind and helpful to people around them.[4]

PRIESTLY WRITERS

In the years after the exile, priests became the important leaders of the people. They were considered the representatives of God and spoke with much power. So it came to pass that the priests compiled other codes of laws (before 450 B.C.). Some of the old laws were joined to new ones. Just as writers in the past used history to teach their religious ideas, so once again the priests, or P, as we shall call these priestly writers, rewrote the Hebrew story to teach their ideas of worship. P wanted to impress upon the Jews the importance of observing certain festivals, ceremonies, and laws. P also used stories to teach his ideas. P believed in one God, but his God seems very exalted and far-off. Obeying certain ceremonial laws became the most important way to worship his God.

In order to encourage the Jews to worship God in the temple of Jerusalem, P wrote long and tiresome descriptions of a tabernacle (Exodus 25-29 and 35-40) and its ceremonies which he said had existed in the days of Moses. The curious thing about these stories of the tabernacle is that P wrote as if the plans had been dictated by Yahweh. These were the ideas P wished the Jews to follow in the temple. Many scholars today do not believe that there ever was such a tabernacle or such elaborate worship of Yahweh in the desert during the

---

[4] Read some of Jesus' criticism of this elaborate kind of worship. Notice how important Jesus felt that man's spirit and attitude toward people were to God in the following: Mark 7:1-9; Luke 19:45-46; Luke 14:1-6; Luke 11:42-43.

time of Moses. Perhaps there had been a crude tent for Yahweh much like those in which desert people themselves lived.

After hundreds of years had passed, Moses became the great hero of the Jews. So the priestly writers probably made over the stories of the past in order to teach new beliefs. People always seem to reverence the past, and as the Jews idealized Moses more and more they grew to think that their beliefs had been given to them by Yahweh through his faithful servant Moses. This proved to be a powerful way to convince the Jews that they should adopt the more elaborate system of priests, ceremonies, and laws for the worship of God. These ideas and customs became increasingly important to the Jews and continued even during and after the days of Jesus. The chief reason for their interruption was the destruction of the great temple in Jerusalem, known as Herod's Temple, by the Roman ruler, Titus, A.D. 70.

THE CHRONICLER WRITES A HISTORY

Nearly two hundred years after the preparation of the elaborate code of the priestly writers, the Chronicler prepared another history of the Hebrews (about 300 B.C.). This story centers all events around the temple and its services in Jerusalem. The books are called I Chronicles and II Chronicles. In many ways they differ from the ideas of the J, E, or D writers in their account of events in the Hebrew story.

More and more the Jewish priests urged the people to obey the religious laws and ceremonies. Obedience to the law was considered by them an important way to honor God and finally the numerous laws became a tiresome burden to religious Jews. If one wished to be truly righteous, he needed to study these laws day and night. Notice the devotion of a loyal Jew in this line from a Psalm:

> Oh how I love Thy Law!
> it is my meditation all the day.
> (Psalm 119:97)

So it came about that pious Jews believed it a way of fellowship with God to meditate on these laws.

OTHER WRITINGS

If you turn to Chart V you will find other books as well as a few chapters in some of the older books of the Old Testament that were written after the Chronicles. One of these later books is Jonah which we have already discovered to be one of the great messages to the Hebrews in the Old Testament.

This gravestone was erected in the time of Jesus over the stone of the ancient Hebrew King Uzziah who reigned about 775 B.C. [II Chronicles 26.] The writing on the stone is Aramaic which was the language spoken in Palestine by Jesus and his friends.

The Old Testament writings were finished about 164 B.C. We have not mentioned all of them because there are so many, but you can find them in the chart.

One of the latest books to be added to the Old Testament is called Daniel. It is very difficult to understand because the writer tells stories of strange visions which the people of that time could understand. The Hebrews were suffering from the cruel ruler, Antiochus Epiphanes, who was trying to crush the Hebrew religion. The writer of Daniel wanted to encourage and comfort his people. He did not sign his name to the book, but used the name of a famous man of the past and wrote as if he were speaking to the people. He seemed to say that someday God would come and establish his kingdom and save the Jewish people.

A GREAT DEBT AND A LONG QUEST

From the ancient library of books in our Bible, millions of people have discovered much about God. In it we have discovered the growth of the Hebrew ideas about God. From some of the Jewish leaders after the exile, Christians and Jews of today have learned much about the nobler meaning of God and of religion. But we must never forget that it is not only to the Hebrews but to many other peoples of the past that we owe gratitude for our religion today. Christians feel an enormous debt of gratitude to Jesus, one of the greatest Jews of all times. The stories about his life and some of his teachings are given in the New Testament of our Bible.

Slowly we are learning that each person must come to know God for himself. We have been helped by the people from the past, but much depends upon our own quest to understand and to know what is the truth. Ideas change because people learn so slowly. But to each person who lives comes the privilege to search and to discover something of God.

> O Brother man! fold to thy heart thy brother;
> Where pity dwells, the peace of God is there;
> To worship rightly is to love each other
> Each smile a hymn, each kindly deed a prayer,
> Follow with reverent steps the great example
> Of Him whose holy work was "doing good";
> So shall the wide earth seem our Father's temple,
> Each loving life a psalm of gratitude.
> Then shall all shackles fall; the stormy clangor
> Of wild war music o'er the earth shall cease;
> And in its ashes plant the tree of peace.
>   —John Greenleaf Whittier

Something to Do

1. Do you have any further plans for the play or pictures telling the story of the Hebrew quest for God?

2. Review Chart V on the order of writing the Old Testament.

3. Try to place the religious ideas of different writers beside their writings in Chart V.

4. Contrast the ideas of the postexilic writers like P, Ezekiel, and the Chronicler, with the ideas of such prophetic writers as Jonah, Ruth, and Second Isaiah. (Read again Chapter XIV.)

5. You may be interested in comparing four codes of laws as recorded by four different Hebrew writers in the Old Testament. Each is supposed to be the code that Moses accepted from Yahweh at Sinai, when Moses made a covenant for the Hebrews with this new god.

J	E	D	Some writers after the exile
Exodus 34: 10-36	Exodus 20:23 to 23:19	Deuteronomy 5:6-21	Exodus 20:3-17

6. What debt do you feel that the Christians of the present owe to the Hebrews and Jews? Write a Psalm or poem or prayer of gratitude.

7. How are you planning to share your discoveries of man's quest for God with some other group?

SECTION FOR THE TEACHER

This material is given to guide those who wish to use this book as a course of study for pupils between the ages of 11 and 18.

A. THE PURPOSE OF THIS COURSE

Inasmuch as the Old Testament is an attempt by many writers living at different periods to present the religious experiences of the Hebrews, it seems desirable to become familiar with some of the various phases of this religious development. The material presented in the Old Testament covers a period of approximately two thousand years. It is important to remember that most of what is written came into existence during the last eight or nine hundred years of that long period and before the time of Jesus. This makes the Old Testament very difficult and confusing, especially when isolated episodes are presented or read without reference to their literary or historical setting.

Fundamental to an understanding of the Bible is an exploratory experience in the growth and development of the Hebrew ideas of God, of worship, and of life. Primitive ideas need to be seen vividly and contrasted with the later teachings of the prophets and of Jesus. In these later teachings may be found some of the loftiest religious views known to man.

Through such an exploration of the Hebrew quest for God, the youth is provided an admirable setting in which to clarify his own thinking about life, worship, and God. In fact, this should become the supreme goal of the whole course—to help youth to work out a religion that will meet its needs in a modern day.

When the Old Testament is read or referred to, this exploratory experience in the development of the Hebrew religion should enable youth to evaluate the material in the light of its original use, as well as to determine its meaning for today.

Attention has been given in the closing chapters to the development of Hebrew literature. From time to time the class should be made aware of some of the Hebrew methods of writing. Frequent illustration will enable the student to see writers at different periods rewriting the Hebrew story and incorporating in it their later ideas of God, of worship, and of laws. Attention should be given to the Hebrew practice of combining different histories into one book and thus placing side by side contrasting and even contradictory ideas. Finally it should be recognized that ancient names such as Abraham, Jacob, or Moses, were frequently used in connection with later customs and ideas. Perhaps this association with such venerable characters lent power and conviction to the views that later writers wished to impress upon the Hebrews.

From time to time attention should be given to the contribution made to the world and particularly to the Christians by the Hebrews in their quest for God. This emphasis, however, should not exclude recognition of the contribution made by many other peoples to our understanding of God.

It is quite probable that some may be confused by the conflicting narratives found in the Old Testament, or there may be difficulty in understanding why a story of creation or a story of Moses or of Abraham describes religious ideas or laws discovered in a period hundreds of years after the time of the person mentioned. In such case, the teacher is advised to make use of the last chapters in the course in order to bring understanding concerning the way the narratives were written.

TEACHER'S PREPARATION

Before teaching this course the teacher is advised to read through the entire book, giving special attention to the last chapters dealing with the development of the Hebrew literature. It will make the guidance of any enterprise selected much easier to work out if the teacher has a good idea of the order of events and writings as outlined in the five charts.

As a background for the course the teacher should become familiar with the following books:

> God and the Social Process, by Louis Wallis.
> The Early Religion of Israel, by Lewis B. Paton.
> The Religion of Israel, by G. A. Barton.

Others are suggested in the Bibliography.

METHOD OF STUDY

Whatever methods are used, it is urged that the purposes of the course be kept constantly in mind by the teacher. The work may meet the needs of the class more continuously if some record is kept by the teacher of individual reactions, questions and environmental background. Perhaps a card for each student is the simplest way to begin. Then, at the time of preparation for each session, these may be read over as a guide for lesson plans.

In the beginning it is important to discover the questions that the group would like answered. As time goes on such questions should become clearer and more significant.

Connections with their own religious ideas and those of long ago may awaken interest on the part of the members of the group. Suggestions are given for the thinking of the pupil at the end of the chapters. These may form a basis for class discussion and study.

When dealing with far-off times and places it is important to locate the places and to understand the words that are used. Pictures of desert life such as are found in the National Geographic Magazine for January, 1937, may be examined and considered as a partial example of nomadic life.

After a vivid glimpse of nomadic life three and a half or four thousand years ago, attention may be directed to the religious practices and ideas of these early Hebrew people.

A brief outline of the Hebrew story has been given in the opening chapter and a few charts of events in later chapters. Perhaps someone may be interested in making a poster on which the dates of these chief events occur. This could be used as an easy reference for class discussion. If space is left at one side of each event or period, some of the religious ideas and practices of the Hebrews may be added from time to time.

If the class period is a short one, the course will take much longer to work out than in a vacation school or in an extended church school period. In schools which provide one and a half or two hour sessions, the period may be divided somewhat as follows:

1. Planning and discussion period for the whole group.

2. Work period in which individuals or committees do research or develop such plans as are necessary for making pictures, a pageant, a book or other activities agreed upon.

3. The climax of each session may well be a worship period for this group or for the department.

After a few sessions of exploration, a decision may be reached concerning the kind of activities in which the class will engage. Some of those listed for the teacher may offer a basis for choice. At the same time, others suggested by members of the class should receive equal consideration.

Frequently there are classes that have had so little experience in planning their work that it takes a considerable time to develop a co-operative participation in a class enterprise. In such cases the teacher may start by offering choices out of a list of suggestions for activity. Then, in the planning and discussion period, committees and individuals may report progress and the opinions of other members of the class may be sought.

Serious and courteous attention to the suggestions and ideas of individual members of the group will do much to encourage a co-operative relationship. If the group feels that its efforts are to be used for some occasion or its discoveries are to be shared with another group, this often adds dignity and provides motivation for initiative and serious work.

In the preparation of slides, a book, posters or a pageant, the teacher needs to be alert to use varied situations which arise for extending knowledge of the Hebrew religion and clarifying the pupils' own religious understanding, as well as making the activity itself a success.

As much encouragement as possible needs to be given to pupil initiative in finding out things. A few books ought to be available to the class for research by individuals or committees or for home study. Students vary in their interests. Therefore any readiness on the part of individual pupils to read or to carry on a meaningful activity should be encouraged.

In the bibliography for the pupil will be found a few books that are starred because of their particular value for this course.

Rapid reading of this course by the pupils should provide a good setting in which to think and to work.

There should be perfect freedom to follow questions and interests discussed in later chapters in this book. For example, it may be necessary to make large use of the chapter on "Places of Worship" or on "Offerings to the Gods" rather early in the course if a pageant or a frieze is to be made.

B. SOME ACTIVITIES TO CLARIFY THINKING

Inasmuch as the story of beginnings in our religion is connected with such a distant past and with such strange and foreign cultures, it seems important to provide activities that will make the life of early people and their religious thinking very vivid and natural for their time.

Activities that give continuity and unity to the work will assure the greatest interest and widest participation. To the class these activities may become the chief consideration, but the teacher should be alert to find opportunities for expansion and growth in knowledge and in religious thinking.

The following activities have been found useful and interesting for this study. A choice should be made after one or two exploratory sessions have been held to locate the interests and needs of the class.

1. Plan a festival or pageant that will show the people in your church how the Hebrews worshiped and thought of God at different periods in their history. Make very clear the progress that took place with reference to such matters as worship, relations between people, and ideas of God. In such an inclusive enterprise, there will be found numerous smaller activities that may involve committees or individuals or at times the whole group. A few subunits are suggested:

a. Rapid reading of this book *How Our Religion Began,* while looking for material to be used in the pageant.

b. More detailed study of the episodes selected as possibilities for the pageant.

c. Consultation with scholars or well-informed persons such as a minister or a Jewish rabbi about these periods in the Hebrew story.

d. Visiting a synagogue and learning about Hebrew customs that may resemble those of Jews after the exile.

e. If scenes are represented in tableau form, creating lines for an interlocutor to read as an interpretation of them.

f. Consulting pictures that are accurate in representing a given period. The *National Geographic Magazine* will often be found useful.

g. Designing and making costumes. This should prove to be a very interesting approach to the Old Testament people.

h. There may be created some scenery which is painted on paper or canvas and fastened to screens.

i. There will be frequent planning meetings in which lists of things to be done will be kept individually or on a large poster where everyone can see it.

j. The historical and religious problems of the periods involved in the pageant will require constant discussion and re-thinking in order to be accurate in the dramatic production.

2. A class book or individual books may be made to show the development and change that took place among the He-brews from nomadic days up to the time of Jesus. Illustrations of change and growth may be shown in their ways of praying, in their offerings, and in their places of worship. Their laws may also be used to illustrate change. Religious customs and ideas connected with war show remarkable development. Drawings, pictures and quotations from the Bible will pro-vide considerable material for a book.

3. Make a frieze for your room showing man's quest to know God. Large pieces of paper may be used for this frieze and arranged side by side after the painting or drawings are complete. These drawings could be placed in a large book after their use in an exhibit or a program. Such episodes could also be drawn on glass and used as slides. Scenes like the follow-ing are suggestive:

a. Nomads worshiping an ēl in an oasis.

b. Nomads making an offering of the first-born lamb.

c. Nomads building a wall around a sacred tree.

d. Moses learning about Yahweh from Jethro.

e. The Hebrews promising to serve Yahweh because of their escape from Egypt.

f. The Hebrews carrying Yahweh in an ark in a battle against the Philistines.

g. The Hebrews worshiping a ba'al at Bethel (a high place of the Canaanites).

h. Solomon building a temple for Yahweh at Jerusalem.

i. The Hebrews declaring Yahweh to be the ba'al of Pales-tine. Naaman moves some of the earth in order to carry Yah-weh to his home.

j. The Hebrews are taught to destroy all of their old "high places" and to worship Yahweh at Jerusalem.

k. Jeremiah tries to teach the Hebrews to give up the sacrifice of their first-born children as gifts to Yahweh.

l. During their exile, the Jews learn from Second Isaiah that they are to be missionaries of one God to all people.

m. Synagogues are built for Jews to study about their religion and about God. There is no sacrifice in them.

n. Spiritual worship is stressed after the exile.

o. Jesus teaches about a God of love and a life of brotherhood.

4. Make some slides by painting or drawing pictures on glass to be used as a program to show another group how the Old Testament was written. Great care should be given to see that the stories around the names of ancient characters were retold to enforce later ideas or practices. The following outline may be of assistance:

a. Nomads seated beside their tents in the desert telling stories to explain floods or other happenings in the life of their ancestors. This went on for hundreds of years.

b. Laws grew up from primitive life in the desert. Perhaps some laws were learned from the code of Hammurabi. Ideas of revenge among desert Hebrews seem very savage.

c. A primitive code of laws probably developed after some of the Hebrews escaped from Egypt.

d. J wrote the first great story of the Hebrews for the people of the southern kingdom of Judah.

e. E wrote a history of the Hebrews for the northern kingdom.

f. Amos denounced the city ways of the Hebrews who had settled in Canaan and came to worship at Bethel.

g. J and E histories were combined.

h. D wrote a new code of laws years after the Hebrews settled in Canaan.

i. During the exile appeared the following writings:

(*1*) The Holiness Code.

(*2*) The joining together of the writings of J, E, and D.

(3) The Second Isaiah challenged the Jews to become missionaries and servants of a God of all people.

(4) Joshua, Judges and Samuel were written.

(5) The Priestly writer outlined plans for a new Temple at Jerusalem giving many laws and elaborate plans for the worship in it.

(6) The Ten Commandments were developed as we have them in Exodus 20.

(7) Ruth is written as a protest against the Hebrew nationalistic laws which opposed intermarriage with other peoples.

(8) Jonah is a story showing the Jews running away from their missionary call to bring other nations to know God.

(9) About 165 B.C. the Old Testament was finished.

5. Tell the story of religion in Egypt in pictures or in a book or in tableaux.

6. Build models or design diagrams to show different altars, sacred places, objects, or temples used by the Hebrews in their worship.

7. Make a picture map to show life in Babylonia, Canaan, Egypt and the desert about 2000 B.C.

8. Build a miniature scene of Hebrew life after they left Egypt and the people were still nomads.

9. Prepare a series of posters to show the changes that gradually took place in the living and in the religion of the Hebrews after they settled in Canaan among the Canaanites. A few suggestions follow:

a. Changing from tents to stone houses.

b. Changing from wanderings with their flocks to an agricultural life where they raised their foods, such as barley, wheat and grapes.

c. Learning to observe agricultural festivals of the Canaanites, such as the "feast of unleavened bread," "the feast of weeks," and "the feast of ingathering."

d. Worshiping the golden calf at the Canaanite shrines of Bethel and other places.

e. Carrying Yahweh in the ark to battles and gradually moving this god away from Mount Sinai.

f. Building a temple for Yahweh at Jerusalem.

g. Worshiping Yahweh at the festivals and the high places instead of other baalim.

h. The Deuteronomist urges the destruction of all high places except Jerusalem.

i. Jeremiah declares that Yahweh is the only God of the Hebrews.

10. Make little plays out of such scenes as the following to reveal religious ideas and practices:

a. The loss of the ark and its return by the Philistines: I Samuel 4, and Jeremiah 26:6. There had been so much worship after the fashion of the Canaanites that the Hebrews were in danger of losing their tribal strength.

b. An ancient story is told of Naaman being healed of leprosy by bathing in the Jordan. He takes earth from Palestine in order to worship Yahweh (II Kings 5:15-17).

c. The Jewish exiles are inspired by an unknown prophet whom we call Second Isaiah to believe that they are God's servants to bring his message to the rest of the world. All of their sufferings are means of making God known to other people. Isaiah 43:22-24; Isaiah 41:8-9; Isaiah 42:2-4; Isaiah 49:1-4; Isaiah 50:4-9; Isaiah 52:15; Isaiah 53:4-6.

d. An episode from Jeremiah revealing his loftier religious ideas as found in such passages as the following: Jeremiah 10:15 and 14:22; Jeremiah 16:17-21; Jeremiah 31:29-34. See Wallis, *God and the Social Process,* for background material on Jeremiah.

11. Make a large poster on which is kept a record of contrasting ideas of God discovered by the class in their study. One column may be labelled "Primitive Ideas" and opposite it another may be labelled "Nobler Ideas."

12. Make a series of tableaux or scenes showing some of the Hebrew prophets such as Elijah, Amos, Isaiah, Jeremiah, and

Second Isaiah. Prepare material for a reader or interlocutor to read from a scroll while these scenes or characters appear. This material may contain important religious ideas and teachings which characterize the prophets in the period of time in which they lived.

C. 1. *Starting the Course*

CHAPTERS I-IV

One of the first steps in this course will be taken by the teacher by making thorough preparation. Besides reading the whole book, it is important to become familiar with some books already suggested for the teacher, as well as some of those to be used by the pupils. Suggestions for activities are made under materials for the teacher and ought to be reviewed from time to time.

Pictures and reading materials should be available from the very beginning to foster interest and to promote thinking. A bibliography found at the close of this book will serve as a guide to the teacher.

In order to make desert life and the viewpoint of these ancient people real, attention may be given to the life of Arabs today as portrayed in the *National Geographic Magazine* for January, 1937, or in other pictures.[1]

After a vivid impression of primitive nomadic life has been created, attention may be given to the viewpoint of Semitic people concerning the world about them. Questions at the close of the first four chapters will provide helpful material for such discussion.

Perhaps a list of discoveries may be made to show the difference between their understanding of nature and ours today. These differences include the shape of the earth, the size and arrangement of the universe, the processes of growth, causes of

[1] The American Colony, Jerusalem, Palestine, has many excellent pictures of desert life.

rain and of flood, the movement of waters, and causes of earth-quakes and of volcanoes.

Out of such a study of contrasts between primitive and modern knowledge, may come a discussion of the differences that would follow in belief about worship and about God.

Some members of the class may wish to read *Finding God*, by G. W. Taylor, to discover certain religious explanations about nature given by early peoples.

The amount of time to be spent on the first four chapters of this course will vary. Some classes may not require four sessions. Others may develop so many questions that a longer period will be used.

By the second session, a test of religious thinking may be given to the class in order to discover the ideas and problems of individuals, as well as to stimulate thinking. Possibly at the close of the course this same test may be repeated in order to discover what progress has been made.

After a clear understanding of the life and religion of the nomadic Hebrews of early days has been developed, the class may study Chart I in Chapter VIII in order to get a perspective on the Hebrew religion record in our Old Testament. This may be printed on a larger chart for more frequent class reference.

Fairly early in the discussions, Chart II in Chapter XI may be copied on a large poster for convenient reference in order to aid the class to grasp something of the development of Hebrew history.

If it is desired, a long border or frieze may be started to mark off important periods in the history of the Hebrews and to record by picture or in writing some of the significant religious ideas or events in each period. This border may be extended as the history unfolds.

From time to time there may be occasion to deal with prejudice against the Jews as this course unfolds. The debt of all

Christians to this great people should be kept constantly in mind. A little book by Basil Mathews, *The Jew and the World Ferment,* will prove a very helpful source of information.

2. *The Egyptian Period*

CHAPTERS V TO VII

To appreciate some of the influences which surrounded the early Hebrews, attention should be given to their Egyptian neighbors and the remarkable civilization which they developed. Fascinating pictures of the monuments which continue to testify to this ancient culture may be enjoyed in many issues of the *National Geographic Magazine.* Several of these numbers are listed in the bibliography.

The Dawn of Conscience, by Breasted, is an invaluable source of material on Egypt for the teacher. Growing out of such reading and the interest of the class, various religious questions and customs may be discussed.

Members of the class may become interested in sections of *The World We Live In,* by Hartman, *How the Present Came from the Past,* by Wells, and *Ancient Egypt,* by Baikie.

Some classes may enjoy co-operating to make one large book on Egypt and its religion. Ideas about the gods, life after death, and religious customs would provide interesting subjects for illustration and discovery. Post card pictures of scenes from ancient writings and temples might be obtained from the British Museum, London, Eng.

Classes that are within reach of museums in the larger cities of the United States may wish to visit them for ideas and for materials.

Inasmuch as Ikhnaton represents such an advanced viewpoint in religion, a play may be created to include him, his family and possibly his son-in-law Tutankhamen.

Some groups may prefer to develop a play from the ancient stories of Joseph found in the book of Genesis. *Ventures in*

Dramatics, by Hulda Niebuhr, will be useful in studying the creation of plays. Additional material on Joseph will be found in *The Religion of Israel,* by G. A. Barton, pages 26-34.

3. *The Worship of Yahweh*

CHAPTERS VIII TO X

Before the teacher attempts to deal with the Hebrew period beginning with the escape from Egypt, it is very important to recognize some of the literary practices of Hebrew writers in order to understand the projection of later ideas into earlier periods of history. Chapters XXIII to XXV should be carefully studied by the teacher as well as such books as *God and the Social Process,* by Wallis, and *The Religion of Israel,* by Barton, particularly pages 68-70.

By this time, the class may be interested in choosing from the suggested list of activities some plan which will give continuity to their study of Hebrew religion in the Old Testament. Slides, posters, models or a play may serve to illustrate the changes in the Hebrew religion. In the *Pilgrim Elementary Teacher* for March, 1933, will be found a fascinating play connected with the ark.

Questions at the close of Chapters VIII to X will be useful in guiding discussions.

Charts I and II should be used in order to get a perspective on the Old Testament story. If plans for the story of Hebrew worship are being made, the class may need to read Chapters XVII and XVIII.

Doubtless there will be need for some knowledge of the material on the writing of the Old Testament. If so the class may be referred to Chapters XXIV and XXV. They may be puzzled to know why so many laws and such elaborate plans for a tabernacle or for worship are ascribed to Moses and the nomadic Hebrews escaping from a life of slavery in Egypt. Chart V may help the class to appreciate the effect of oral tradition upon the

written story which was arranged by varied writers centuries
later.

Such topics as follow may be included in the class discussion:

  a. Possible reasons for the Hebrew escape from Egypt.
     Stories and legends which probably grew up around
     the event.
  b. The custom of worshiping the god of a given locality.
  c. Reasons for the great devotion of the Hebrews to their
     new-found god, Yahweh.
  d. The way the later Hebrews explained their escape and
     the part of Yahweh in it.
  e. Our reasons for believing Yahweh was a volcano god.
  f. The custom of carrying Yahweh in arks.
  g. The qualities and powers ascribed to Yahweh.
  h. The contrast between Yahweh and the God of Jesus or
     of the prophets after the exile.

The ark

Most teaching in the church school concerning the ark has
given the interpretation of the priestly viewpoint of the Old
Testament. The priestly writers were writing in a period after
500 B.C. when the Hebrews wished to focus attention upon an
"ark of testimony" used in the temple. These writers simply
ignore the numerous sacred boxes of the older historical writings and idealize and exalt the idea of a single "box of Yahweh." To understand this complicated and difficult problem,
the teacher is referred to *Ephod and Ark*, by William R. Arnold, issued as an extra number of the *Harvard Theological
Review*.

Arnold says, "The imaginative writer of the period, when
treating of the early days of Israel's history, hesitates to project
backwards into the days of Moses and Joshua just such an individual box of Yahweh as had accompanied the armies of Saul
and David in later times. So we must interpret the role of the

imaginary box of Yahweh in Numbers 10:33, 35, 36 and 14:44 and in the pre-exilic stratum of Joshua 3-8.

"Not until some time after the temple of Solomon had been swept away—hardly much before 500 B.C.—did it occur to any-one to question the original purpose of the Solomonic box. This transition from the box of historical fact and historical imagination to the box of Jewish dogma was effected by means of two correlated sets of interpolations, the one in Deuteron-omy 10:1-5, the other in 1 Kings 8:9, 21. The original stories of the Sinaitic tables of stone had nothing to say about the box—naturally enough, for public laws are not put under a bushel. And the original story of the box of the Solomonic temple had nothing to say about the Sinaitic tables of stone in Deuteronomy 10, and the Sinaitic tables of stone were thrust into the box of the Solomonic temple in I Kings."[2]

In the legends among the Abyssinian Christians is one en-titled the Tigre legend. This legend claims that Menelik took the ark of the covenant with him from Jerusalem and brought it to Axum, where it is now supposed to be in the sanctuary of the church. The details of this superstition are crude. Probably these sacred stones go back to the times of paganism. When Mary's ark reached Axum, it was said to Satan, "Mary had come to thee." In the same way as the Philistines said when the ark of Yahweh reaches the camp of the Israelites "Yahweh is come into the camp" (I Samuel 4:7).[3]

4. Worship in Canaan

CHAPTERS XI AND XII

Chart I revealing the development of religion among the Hebrews should be reviewed in order to see the relation of the new experiences in Canaan to their past.

Attention should be given to the movement of the god, Yah-

[2] Arnold, Wm. R., *Ephod and Ark,* issued as an extra number of the *Harvard Theological Review*, published by the Harvard University Press, Cambridge, 1917, p. 139.
[3] Dr. E. Littmann, *Bibliotheca Abessinicam.* The University Library, Princeton, N. J., 1904, p. 37.

weh, into Canaan in the ark, as well as to the changes in his powers and position as the centuries passed. It is helpful to compare earlier ideas of Yahweh with these later ones.

Charts II and III offer a brief survey of the Hebrew story.

A list of changes in the experience and ideas of the Hebrews after they settled in Canaan may be made. Contrasts with nomadic practices should be considered.

Some classes may enjoy making a play out of the material on Amos. The teacher should read Wallis, *God and the Social Process*, pages 180ff., and *Amos Studies*, by Julian Morgenstern, Hebrew Union College, Cincinnati, O., 1936.

Questions at the close of the chapters will guide the discussion.

Out of the materials may be selected illustrations for slides, posters, or models to tell the story of the Hebrew quest for God.

5. *Hebrew Life after the Exile*

CHAPTERS XIII TO XV

The pupils should be encouraged to read the story in this book as well as *How the Great Religions Began*, by Gaer, and parts of *From Desert to Temple*, by Whitman. The teacher will also benefit by reading this last book. Excellent descriptions of the invasions of Palestine by Egypt, Assyria, and Babylonia will be found on pages 263 to 283 of Wallis, *God and the Social Process*.

Charts I, II, III, and IV need to be studied very carefully. If a frieze or border is being created to illustrate significant events in different periods, there will be some additions to it.

New materials will be needed for the slides, posters or play, which reveal the Hebrew quest for God.

The following topics deserve attention:

(*a*) Reasons for the exile.
(*b*) The people who were being carried away.

(c) Origin of the Jewish hostility towards the Samaritans.

(d) The attitude of many of the exiles towards Jerusalem.

(e) The significant teachings about God that develop during the exile. The contrast between these ideas and earlier ones.

(f) The meaning of the suffering of the exiles to certain Jewish leaders.

(g) The lofty teaching by the writer of Jonah to the exclusive and nationalistic Jews.

(h) The growth of the prejudice of the Jews towards foreigners and the great teaching of the writer of Ruth.

(i) A comparison of the nobler ideas of God during the exile with those of Jesus.

Some classes may wish to create and to present a play out of the story of Ruth and to use it to show that because God is a Father of all people, they should live as brothers. Note Mark 12:29-31.

Perhaps a dramatic setting could be created by the class to show the reaction of the Jews to the message delivered by the writer of Jonah. Some help will be found in Bewer's *Literature of the Old Testament*, pages 403 to 405.

6. *Hebrew Worship*

CHAPTERS XVI TO XX

These chapters will serve as a vivid and intensive survey of the religious growth of the Hebrews as revealed in the long history so briefly sketched in the preceding chapters. If this material is used in connection with Chart I, it should serve to make more vivid any plans under way to illustrate the story of the Hebrew quest for God.

Tableaux of the different ways of worship may be created and explained by an interlocutor. This could be made into a program and given for the older pupils of a church school or for a parents' group.

During the discussion of worship the class may benefit by making a list of nobler reasons for offerings in worship.

Similarly attention should be given to the differences in prayers. Consider the changes that come in prayers as nobler ideas of God develop. It would be interesting to read some prayers and then decide on the worshipers' ideas of God.

Chapters XVIII and XIX may be used to develop further any pageantry or drawings that are under way. If no previous use has been made of this material, different members of the class may select ways of worship or places of worship as illustrations to be used on slides. Glass the size of lantern slides may be coated with gelatin and used to paint scenes or to make drawings in India ink. After the slides have been made, they may be shown by the class as a lantern lecture to some other group.

If possible, a trip to an orthodox synagogue should be taken in connection with the study of places of worship. Perhaps the class may be interested in reproducing a service in the synagogue such as Jesus would have experienced in his day. *With Jewish Child in Home and Synagogue,* by Levinger, will provide interesting material for class reading. The teacher will find useful material in Edersheim's *Life and Times of Jesus,* pages 440ff.

Chart IV may provide more data for the chronological border or frieze if it has been started.

Questions at the close of the chapters will be fruitful for class discussion. The story of the Sabbath and of our Sunday may be better understood by following the questions at the close of Chapter XX.

7. *Spirits and the Dead*

CHAPTER XXI

The teacher will be aided greatly by reading portions of *The Religion of Israel,* by G. A. Barton, and of *Experience with the Supernatural,* by S. J. Case.

Questions at the close of Chapter XXI will be of help in the class discussion.

Whatever viewpoints there are in the class about immortality, it may be valuable to consider the ongoing effect of the behavior of people, especially that which is in accord with the truth about life and that which promotes love and goodness. Study the significance of I John 4:12, I Corinthians 3:16, and John 4:24. What is meant by the statement: "Where love is, there God is"? What part does God have in the ongoing effects of goodness in the lives of people? What difference has Jesus' life in Palestine made in the world during the hundreds of years that have elapsed since that time?

If there are enterprises of painting, pageantry or drawing under way, they may need further attention. Perhaps each individual is ready to explain his particular work to the rest of the class and in this way gather suggestions to unify the whole plan.

8. *Jesus Reveals the Power of Man's Noblest Concept of God*

CHAPTER XXII

If possible, the teacher should read such a book as *The Religion of Jesus*, by Bundy.

Encouragement in reading the Gospel of Mark at a single sitting may help the class to feel the drama of Jesus' wonderful life. *How One Man Changed the World,* by Blanchard, is a superior story of Jesus, written in an interesting way for younger people.

Evidence may be gathered to show how Jesus showed love, not merely in word but in deed. His ideas of God and his ways of worship may be summarized. Biblical references to Jesus in Chapters XVI and XVIII may be useful here.

What difference should it make in the behavior of people if they believe that God supports intelligent ways of love and brotherhood in all of life's relation? What difference does it make when people believe in the germ theory of disease?

Would it make a difference if people came to believe in a law of love operating as constantly as laws of disease? What difference did belief in a way of love seem to make in the life of Jesus?

Summarize the nobler ideas of God which have been emphasized by Jews and by Jesus since the exile. Compare these with earlier ideas.

Perhaps the test given in the first part of this course may be taken again in order to discover any changes in the thinking of members of the class. This may serve as a review, as well as a way to clear up any problems which have arisen.

9. *Sources of Knowledge of the Hebrews*

CHAPTERS XXIII TO XXV

Any plans which are under way in the preparation of a special program to share discoveries about our religion, made in this course, should be completed.

An interesting method of studying the closing chapters (XXIII to XXV) on the sources of our knowledge of the Hebrews might be through the making of slides as suggested under "Some Activities to Clarify Thinking." An outline is given, but this should in no way prevent originality and pupil planning.

The teacher will doubtless need to study more in detail about the growth of the Old Testament. Many helps will be found in *God and the Social Process*, by Wallis, especially pages 246 to 266, and *The Religion of Israel*, by Barton. Particularly useful is a little inexpensive book by Blunt, *Israel before Christ*.

Chart V will serve as a practical survey of the Old Testament literature. This may be printed on a large poster for class reference. It may be of interest to compare it with the arrangement of the books as we have them in the Old Testament today.

Some classes may enjoy finding and underscoring with colored pencils the J and the E records of such stories as those of Abram, Isaac, Joseph, the plagues in Egypt, or the experiences at Sinai. Some exact references are given in Chapters V and VI of Bewer's *Literature of the Old Testament*. These chapters will be very enriching for the teacher. Another plan would be to cut out the sections of each writer from an old Bible and paste them together to show the way the J and the E story may have read before they were joined together.

Material on the Chronicler will be found in Bewer's *Literature of the Old Testament*, pages 286 to 302.

Questions at the close of each chapter will be useful for class discussion.

To avoid a too tedious and detailed account of the Old Testament literature, some books are not treated in this course. Certain materials from the Psalms are quoted, but little has been written about this form of literature.

The Psalms

References are given for the teacher and will enable her to carry on whatever study seems desirable. Chapter XX in Bewer, *Literature of the Old Testament,* gives considerable help.

The Psalms were probably collected after the exile, much as we have them. Their development represents a long period of time. It is fascinating to read them in connection with circumstances in history out of which they may have come.

The Psalms were used in the temple services in connection with the feasts and sacrifices. They were sung by a temple choir, accompanied by temple music, and responses were chanted by the people. In Psalm 150 may be found a list of these musical instruments. In later times the Psalms were used in the synagogue service.

Some scholars believe that there was a great festival of the new year (before the exile) when the god, Yahweh, was enthroned. At this time, a procession marched about the temple or the city of Jerusalem carrying the ark. The ark was brought to the temple and Yahweh was enthroned in the sanctuary. It is believed that Psalms 24, 96, 97, 98, 99 and 132 were used in this ceremony of the enthronement of Yahweh.

Certain Psalms were used for private devotions. Psalm 139 deals with a later belief in one god. Such a Psalm as 50 was probably chanted by a priest in the temple as the voice of God speaking to the people.

Psalms 19:7ff., and 119 were created to praise newly adopted laws that probably came into use after the exile.

Psalms 50 and 51 represent a later revolt against animal sacrifices in the worship of God. Reading as though it had been tacked on by some writer devoted to temple sacrifice, we find 51:18, 19.

A fascinating study of the Psalms could be made by discovering the different ideas of God and His will for the relations of people to each other.

BIBLIOGRAPHY FOR THE TEACHER ONLY

Note: The asterisks are before books of great value for the teacher.

BAIKIE, JAMES, *Life of the Ancient East.* New York: The Macmillan Company, 1923.

*BARTON, G. A., *The Religion of Israel.* New York: The Macmillan Company. Valuable reference on the growth of the Hebrew religion.

————, *Semitic Origins.*

*————, *Archaeology and the Bible,* 1937. Many useful pictures.

*BEWER, J. A., *The Literature of the Old Testament in Its Historical Development.* New York: Columbia University Press, Revised Edition.

BLUNT, A. W. F., *Israel before Christ.* New York: Oxford University Press, 1932.

*BREASTED, J. H., *The Dawn of Conscience.* New York: Charles Scribner's Sons.

————, *The Conquest of Civilization.* New York: Harper & Brothers. Valuable pictures and history of ancient civilization.

BROWNE, LEWIS, *The Graphic Bible.* New York: The Macmillan Company, 1928. Excellent graphic maps.

CALKINS, RAYMOND, *Jeremiah the Prophet.* New York: The Macmillan Company, 1930.

*CASE, S. J., *Experience with the Supernatural.* New York: Century Co., 1929.

*FOSDICK, H. E., *A Guide to Understanding the Bible.* New York: Harper & Brothers, 1938. Essential to a teacher of this course.

KENNETT, ROBERT HATCH, *Ancient Hebrew Social Life and Custom as Indicated in Law, Narrative and Metaphor.* London: Oxford University Press, 1933.

LEVINGER, ELMA and LEE, *The Story of the Jew.* New York. Bloch Publishing Co.

MOEHLMAN, HENRY CONRAD, *The Story of the Ten Commandments.* New York: Harcourt, Brace & Co., 1928.

MATHEWS, BASIL, *The Jew and the World Ferment.* New York: Friendship Press, 1935.

National Geographic Magazine.
    September, 1913, Vol. XXIV, No. 9, pp. 962-1018.
    September, 1926, Vol. L, No. 3, pp. 312-355.
    December, 1926, Vol. L, No. 6, pp. 649-728.
    December, 1927, Vol. LI, No. 6, pp. 708-743.
    October, 1930, Vol. LVII, No. 4, pp. 476-516.
    July, 1933, Vol. LXIV, No. 1, pp. 96-126.

PATON, LEWIS B., *The Early Religion of Israel.* Boston: Houghton Mifflin Co.

PETRIE, FLINDERS, *The Arts and Crafts of Ancient Egypt.* Edinburgh: McClourg & Co., 1910.

PETERS, JOHN P., *The Psalms as Liturgies.* New York: Macmillan Company, 1930.

POTTER, C. F., *Story of Religion.* New York: Simon and Schuster, 1929.

QUIBELL, MRS. H. A., *Egyptian History and Art.* New York: The Macmillan Co.

RASHWAN, CARL R., *Black Tents of Arabia.* Boston: Little, Brown & Co. Good desert pictures.

SMITH, J. M. POWIS, *The Origin and History of Hebrew Law.* Chicago: University of Chicago Press, 1931.

WALLIS, LOUIS, *God and the Social Process.* Chicago: University of Chicago Press, 1935.

WOOLLEY, SIR LEONARD, *Abraham.* New York: Charles Scribner's Sons, 1936.

TECHNIQUES OF TEACHING AND COURSES OF STUDY

Some descriptions of units carried on by other teachers[1]

ACHESON, EDNA L., "The Ark of Yahweh," *Pilgrim Elementary Teacher*. Boston: Pilgrim Press, March and April 1933.

BAXTER, EDNA M., *A Friendship Enterprise with Our Jewish Neighbors,* Unit No. 4. Boston: Pilgrim Press.

COMIUS, HARRY L., *The Life of the Early Hebrews,* Edited by the New York Committee for School Extension. A course for Jewish synagogues.

ELLIS, EMILY F., *The Life and Religion of the Early Hebrews,* Unit I. Boston: Beacon Press, Inc. Describes a unit.

FOULGER, T. R., *The Hebrew Quest for God,* Form VI. Madras, India: Christian Literature Society for India.

MALONEY, GERTRUDE, *Life of the Early Hebrews.* New York: Bureau of Publications, Teachers College, Columbia University.

PICKENS, IDA M., *Egypt.* New York: Bureau of Publications, Teachers College, Columbia University.

WHITMAN, ELEANOR W., *From Desert to Temple,* Teacher's edition. Boston: Beacon Press. Scholarly course of study on Hebrew history for high juniors or for intermediates. Valuable for reference.

ZELIGS, D. F., *When We Were Nomads.* New York: Bureau of Publications, Teachers College, Columbia University.

[1] The teacher's attention is called to the fact that some of these units ignore the idea of religious development among the Hebrews. They are better in customs than in the area of religion.

BIBLIOGRAPHY FOR THE PUPIL'S USE

Note: The asterisk indicates high value.

I. WRITING AND RECORDS

CHIERA, EDWARD, *They Wrote on Clay*. Chicago: University of Chicago Press, 1938.

CLODD, EDWARD, *The Story of the Alphabet*. New York: D. Appleton-Century Co., 1913.

MAXWELL, MARJORIE, *The Story of Books*. New York: Harper & Brothers, 1928.

*WELLS, M. E., *How the Present Came from the Past*, Vol. II. New York: The Macmillan Co., 1932.

II. HISTORY OF THE RACE

COFFMAN, RAMON, *The Child's Story of the Human Race*. New York: Dodd, Mead & Co., 1924.

HARTMAN, GERTRUDE, *The World We Live In*. New York: The Macmillan Co., 1931. For intermediate age.

HILLYER, V. M., *The Child's History of the World*. New York: The Century Co., 1924. For junior age.

VAN LOON, H. W., *The Story of Mankind*. New York: Boni & Liveright, 1923.

*WELLS, M. E., *How the Present Came from the Past*. New York: The Macmillan Company, Vols. I, II, 1932.

III. EVOLUTION OF THE WORLD

ERLEIGH, EVA, *In the Beginning*. New York: Doubleday, Page & Co., 1926.

REED, W. MAXWELL, *The Earth for Sam*. Harcourt, Brace & Co., Inc., 1930.

*RIFKIN, LILLIAN, *Our Planet and the Earth*. Boston: Lothrop, Lee & Shepard Co., 1934. Useful for pictures.

IV. ANCIENT EGYPT

BAIKIE, REV. JAMES, *Ancient Egypt*. London: A. & C. Black, Ltd., 1929.

KELLY, R. T., *Peeps at Many Lands,* School Edition. New York: The Macmillan Co, 1916.

MILLS, D., *The Book of the Ancient World.* New York: G. P. Putnam's Sons, 1923.

POTTER, C. F., *The Story of Religion.* 1929. New York: Simon and Schuster. Contains story of Ikhnaton.

National Geographic Magazine, Washington, D. C.
**December, 1909, Vol. XX.
September, 1913, Vol. XXIV.
February, 1916, Vol. XXIX.
May, 1923, Vol. XLIII.
March, 1926, Vol. L.
September, 1926, Vol. L.
December, 1927, Vol. LI.

V. RELIGIOUS IDEAS

*CLODD, EDWARD, F. R. A. S., *The Childhood of the World.* London: Sunday School Association, 37 Norfolk St., Strand, 1914.

GAER, JOSEPH, *How the Great Religions Began.* New York: Robert M. McBride & Co., 1929.

**National Geographic Magazine,* Washington, D. C., January, 1920, Vol. XXXVIII.

TAYLOR, G. W., *Finding God.* London: St. Christopher Press, 1929. Obtained Through The Macmillan Co., New York.

VI. JEWISH CUSTOMS AND FESTIVALS

LEVINGER, ELMA E., *In Many Lands.* New York: 31 West 31st St., Bloch Publishing Co., 1923. Gives stories of the Jews keeping their festivals in varied lands.

———, *With Jewish Child in Home and Synagogue.* New York: Bloch Publishing Co., 1935.

VII. JESUS

BLANCHARD, F. Q., *How One Man Changed the World.* Boston: Pilgrim Press, 1928.

COFFEE AND COWEN, *Family Portrait.* New York: Random House, 1939.